THE STORY OF THE

ODYSSEY

THE STORY OF THE
ODYSSEY

STEPHEN V. TRACY

PRINCETON UNIVERSITY PRESS · PRINCETON, NEW JERSEY

Grateful acknowledgment is made for permission to reprint copyrighted
material from The "Odyssey" of Homer: A Modern Translation
by Richmond Lattimore. Copyright © 1965, 1967 Richmond Lattimore.
Reprinted by permission of Harper & Row, Publishers, Inc.

Library of Congress Cataloging-in-Publication Data
Tracy, Stephen V., 1941–
The story of the Odyssey / Stephen V. Tracy.
p. cm.
Includes bibliographical references.
ISBN 0-691-06855-0 (alk. paper)—ISBN 0-691-01494-9
(pbk. : alk. paper)
1. Homer. Odyssey. I. Title.
PA4167.T7 1990
883'.01—dc20   90-34573

This book has been composed in Linotron Palatino
Princeton University Press books are printed on acid-free paper
and meet the guidelines for permanence and durability of the
Committee on Production Guidelines for Book Longevity
of the Council on Library Resources

Printed in the United States of America

5 7 9 10 8 6

FOR

Steve, Erik, Ben, and Mark

CONTENTS

PREFACE

WHY ANOTHER book on the *Odyssey*? Quite frankly because there is none like this one in English and there is a need for it. The idea for this book was planted by one of my students at the American School of Classical Studies, Lisa Cox, during a drive to Delphi and Mt. Parnassos on a snowy winter's day in early 1982. Almost two years later I began writing out of a conviction that such a book was needed and as a way of working myself out of a period of listless inactivity (my own not-very-pleasant trip to Lotos land) caused by a tragedy in my immediate family. I have learned much about the *Odyssey* from writing this book; it will in turn be gratifying to me if others can learn something from reading it. One note of advice to beginning readers: always read Homer first and keep returning to him. Do not let yourself be overwhelmed by the sheer mass of the secondary literature.

Apart from one three-month period released from teaching duties, I have had no specific support for the writing of this book. I have, therefore, had to work on it in spurts—the first in late 1983 and spring of 1984, the next in January to May of 1985, and finally in the summers of 1986 and 1988. The only thanks to be recorded, then, are personal ones. Madonna Alessandro kindly entered on the computer an early draft of the whole. Thomas Loening and June Allison read the manuscript in its entirety and offered many helpful comments. I owe probably more than I can know to my teachers at Harvard, especially to the late Cedric Whitman, to John Finley, and to my mentor Sterling Dow, who has had a long-time interest in the Bronze Age and in Homer. I have certainly learned most from teaching the poem at various levels for the past twenty years. To all of my students, many of whom by

their questions and interpretations helped me to understand
the poem better, I owe a great debt of thanks, not least for
their patience. Lastly, to June, whose love and gentle wit
have sustained me—you have truly shown the wisdom in
Odysseus' words to Nausicaa (*Odyssey* 6.182–84):

οὐ μὲν γὰρ τοῦ γε κρεῖσσον καὶ ἄρειον,
ἢ ὅθ᾽ ὁμοφρονέοντε νοήμασιν οἶκον ἔχητον
ἀνὴρ ἠδὲ γυνή·

(Nothing is more powerful and better than when
a husband and wife, harmonious in their thoughts, make
a home together.)   (My trans.)

As one of the most entertaining adventure stories of all
time, the *Odyssey* deserves to be read and re-read by every
person, young and old. I, a proud father and uncle, fondly
dedicate this study to my sons and nephew with the heartfelt
wish that their own voyages to Ithaca will have the richness
of Homer's.

St. Augustine Beach, Florida
September 1988

Postscript: G. E. Dimock's *The Unity of the "Odyssey"* (Am-
herst, 1989) appeared too late for me to take account of it.

INTRODUCTION

THE *Odyssey* has something for everyone; it is a highly entertaining adventure story that features witches and one-eyed giants, damsels in distress, love affairs, etc. The bad guys get what is coming to them; the good guys win out in the end. Moreover, the hero is a likable, slightly roguish character. In short, the story and the hero are approachable; they appeal to audiences. But the poem is not simply a light tale of adventure; it deals with the basic problems that all men face, and that is why it remains one of the most read and well-known poems in world literature. What, then, is the *Odyssey* about? Each critic and reader must eventually respond for himself to this difficult question. If pressed, I would answer life and death, home and family—the mainsprings that motivate human beings. Few poets have dealt so effectively with these themes. On the surface the *Odyssey* recounts the adventures of a warrior on his return home to his family from a great war. But Homer invests this return with unusual meaning; he shows us in the starkest terms the difficulty of going home. Situations do not remain the same; even a simple return home is fraught with danger, as everyone knows who has tried it. For an heroic warrior, however, the return can be a perilous ordeal—the transition from a world of killing to one where the rule of law obtains is not an easy one; the poet suggests, in fact, that one must die and be reborn. In the course of his journeys Odysseus also confronts the basic fact of the human condition. Humans are mortal—they cannot be immortal—and must die. Death gives life its meaning; indeed the poet makes it clear that to live forever would strip life of its significance. Though death is inevitable, he suggests in the underworld passages that it is nothing to be desired. Life with all its sufferings is vastly preferable.

One should never, therefore, give in to the various temptations to stop living. Such ideas sound trite indeed when stated in declarative sentences. Fortunately, poets use a different language. These themes (and others) receive expression during the course of a richly woven tale; below, I attempt to trace them out by following Homer's narrative thread.

To paraphrase the late H.D.F. Kitto, authors tell their stories, if it is stories they are telling, with certain words and not others and in a certain order. They usually know what they are doing and it is the business of a critic to try to appreciate what they have done, not to second-guess them or criticize them for what they have not done.[1] It is the purpose of this book to describe what Homer has done and to try to suggest why what he has done makes one of the best tales ever told. It takes as its model E. T. Owen's sensitive *The Story of the "Iliad."* I intend this book for university undergraduates who will, alas, be Greekless and, in many cases, more lamentably, will be approaching the *Odyssey* for the first time. I thus provide translations of all passages[2] and, lest one daunt the uninitiated, have included only a few footnotes as guides for further reading in English.[3] Of course I hope that this book will also be of use to my colleagues, advanced students and teachers.

[1] Kitto, *Poiesis*, 1–32, esp. 30–32.

[2] The Greek text is that of the Oxford Classical Text of Homer, vols. 3 and 4, ed. T. W. Allen (Oxford: Clarendon Press, 1917, 1919). The translations of phrases and sentences in the narrative are the author's. Translations of the separately quoted Greek passages, except where marked as by the author, are by Richmond Lattimore from *The "Odyssey" of Homer: A Modern Translation*, copyright © 1965, 1967 Richmond Lattimore, reprinted by permission of Harper and Row, Publishers, Inc.

[3] These notes primarily refer to discussions that go into more depth than is possible in a study of this kind. I have not attempted to indicate systematically alternate opinions or points of controversy. On certain matters that seem basic, however, I have tried to make reference to other points of view so that the beginner will be aware not only that other opinions exist, but that there is heated controversy on some issues. To rehearse that controversy is not the purpose of this book.

I do not attempt to discuss in this study any of the matters that generally are subsumed under the words "the Homeric question," but it is fair to state my general view of the matter. I assume that there was one author (whom I see no reason not to call Homer) who used the aid of writing to create the poem.[4] As a student of C. H. Whitman and, to a lesser extent, of A. B. Lord, this is a view to which I have come reluctantly because it best accounts for what I find in the text.[5] There is no position on this difficult matter, I might add, that does not have its problems. I also think that we have Homer's text essentially as he left it to us. There are some interpolated lines, but, to quote the most influential translator of Homer in English, Richmond Lattimore, I do not know which ones they are.[6] I do identify in what follows some lines in the eleventh and twenty-third books that I think are quite certainly interpolated. Nevertheless, the poem as we have it has not suffered large-scale alteration; it has a manifest artistic integrity, which I trust the words that follow will, at least in part, elucidate.[7]

The *Odyssey* falls naturally into tetrads, i.e., units of four books: books one to four present the story of Telemachus; in books five to eight Odysseus leaves Calypso and encounters the Phaeacians; nine to twelve contain Odysseus' first-person

[4] Most scholars regard Homer as an oral poet who composed without the aid of writing. The classic presentation of this point of view is by A. B. Lord, *The Singer of Tales*, esp. 141–57. For further discussion, see G. S. Kirk, *Homer and the Oral Tradition*, esp. 113–45. Among scholars who hold that writing was used may be mentioned Adam Parry, "Have We Homer's *Iliad*?"; G. P. Goold, "The Nature of Homeric Composition"; and Alfred Heubeck in his general introduction to volume 1 of *A Commentary on Homer's "Odyssey,"* esp. 12–13.

[5] Finnegan, particularly in chapter 3 of *Oral Poetry*, has shown that oral poetry has wider possibilities than I am accustomed to believing; perhaps after all an oral poet can exercise the minute control that I perceive in these two very long and very great epic poems.

[6] Lattimore, *The "Odyssey" of Homer*, 23 n. 3.

[7] On the difficulties facing the critic of Homer's poetry, see Amory, "The Gates of Horn and Ivory," 36–39, and Hainsworth, "The Criticism of an Oral Homer."

narrative of his wanderings; in books thirteen to sixteen Odysseus and Telemachus return to Ithaca and are reunited; books seventeen to twenty bring Odysseus to his palace and depict Penelope's decision to set the contest of the bow; twenty-one to twenty-four show Odysseus taking his revenge and recovering his rightful place as king. Following these clear-cut divisions of the poet, I have divided this book into six chapters, one on each tetrad. For convenience, my discussion of each tetrad follows the book divisions that have come down to us. I intend no implication that these are the author's. Whoever made them, however, probably the scholars at the library in Alexandria during the third and second centuries B.C.,[8] did so with a high degree of sensitivity to the composer's divisions of subject matter.

[8] For the activities of the Alexandrian scholars and a different view of when the book divisions were made, see Stephanie West in Heubeck et al., *A Commentary on Homer's "Odyssey,"* 1: 39–48.

THE STORY OF THE

ODYSSEY

CHAPTER 1

Books One to Four

THE FIRST FOUR books of the *Odyssey* deal with Telemachus, the son of the hero. They come, or should come, as a considerable surprise to anyone encountering the poem for the first time. The title of the poem in Greek, *Odysseia*, means story of Odysseus and surely leads us to expect to meet right from the opening the hero whose name graces the title. Homer clearly took some pleasure as a poetic craftsman in postponing for four books the entrance of his hero. It is a *tour de force* surpassed only by the *Iliad*, where he introduces Achilles and then removes him for two-thirds of the poem, yet still manages to make the entire epic center on the absent hero. Once we get over our surprise, we should realize with delight what an effective beginning these four books make.

They present to us in the most vivid terms Ithaca, Odysseus' goal, and the dire need for him at home. His wife besieged with suitors, his son disconsolate, his father withdrawn to the country in grief—his entire house threatens to fall. This is the background for Odysseus' tale. This tetrad then establishes in a leisurely fashion several of the major themes of the poem, freeing the poet when he gets to Odysseus to concentrate on the hero. These themes are primarily the need for the sons of heroes to grow up worthy of their fathers, eating/drinking (especially in the context of entertaining guests) as a touchstone of behavior, and the journey as a symbol of growth.

In Telemachus' search for knowledge of his father, the journey also soon becomes a metaphor for the search for identity. Telemachus begins by seeking news of his father, whether he is alive or not, but ends by gaining understanding of his father. Since to the Greeks one's father in particular determines one's identity—their very habit of name-giving (i.e., one is always "so and so, *son* of so and so") reveals how ingrained in their psyche this thought pattern was—knowledge of one's father becomes ultimately self-knowledge; by knowing his father Telemachus will know himself. Odysseus' journeys, though more extreme, are also ones of self-discovery. Odysseus comes to understand who he is, in the sense of what it means to be a man and to die. He comes, as we shall see, to understand his mortality.

At the beginning, Telemachus in Ithaca keeps company with the unruly suitors who, by their constant feasting, are literally devouring Odysseus' household. In terms of eating and drinking Telemachus has no positive role model at home and must journey outside to learn proper behavior. It is no accident, then, that he finds Nestor sacrificing and Menelaos celebrating a wedding feast, two of the most important occasions for feasting in the ancient world. These contemporaries of his father, then, give Telemachus proper models of behavior but just as importantly they give him firsthand experience of his father's world. Menelaos in particular has experienced a return very similar to that of Odysseus. To begin with the son also emphasizes unmistakably that this poem deals with family in its largest sense and in that particularly Mediterranean sense of defining its continuance by male heirs. Sons have paramount importance.[1]

The gods, Athena first and foremost, take a particular interest in Odysseus and his family. Athena persuades Zeus at the opening of book one to agree to Odysseus' return; disguised as Mentes and then Mentor, she advises Telemachus on Ithaca and then guides him to Pylos; and, lastly, at the end of book four she reassures Penelope about Telemachus'

[1] On Telemachus, see H. W. Clarke, "Telemachus and the *Telemacheia*."

safe return. Homer carefully depicts from the opening her concern for Odysseus' entire family. In the case of Telemachus, Athena instigates action, breaks the impasse caused by his youthful lack of confidence, and guides him a short way. Her departures mark steps in his growing independence.

BOOK ONE

Homer begins his tale rapidly. After a ten-line proem in which he calls upon the Muse to sing the return (*nostos*) of a hero from Troy who had many adventures, the poet straight away gives his story a divine background (11–95). The first person we hear speaking is Zeus himself (32ff.). What more effective device could there be to persuade us of the importance of the action and the hero than to show the Olympian gods personally involved? Moreover, the use of Zeus allows the poet to be arbitrary without seeming to be. Zeus can bring up any subject he likes. Who would question it? Here he just happens to be thinking about Aigisthos and remarks that men blame the gods, but it is, in fact, they who bring destruction on themselves through their own recklessness. Aigisthos' death at the hands of Orestes is his example. Homer here, in a seemingly casual manner, introduces the story of Agamemnon, a story that he will use repeatedly as a paradigm of behavior for both Telemachus and Odysseus. He also establishes at the outset the important principle that men are responsible for their actions. We have already had intimations of this from lines 6–9 of the proem, where we learn that Odysseus' companions died because they ate the cattle of the Sun. It will not be long before we hear about the suitors and their eating habits (91–92). First, however, the story of Odysseus must be set in motion.

Athena takes the opportunity offered by Zeus' musings about human affairs to bring up Odysseus. See particularly lines 48–49:

ἀλλά μοι ἀμφ᾽ Ὀδυσῆϊ δαΐφρονι δαίεται ἦτορ,
δυσμόρῳ, ὃς δὴ δηθὰ φίλων ἄπο πήματα πάσχει

(But the heart in me is torn for the sake of wise Odysseus,
unhappy man, who still, far from his friends, is suffering.)

The assonance and alliteration on delta and pi sounds in
these two lines suggest Athena's indignation. She tries to put
Zeus on the defensive as she closes her speech (60–62) by
suggesting with two rhetorical questions that he has it in for
Odysseus. Zeus responds (64–65) with two rhetorical questions of his own:

τέκνον ἐμόν, ποῖόν σε ἔπος φύγεν ἕρκος ὀδόντων.
πῶς ἂν ἔπειτ᾽ Ὀδυσῆος ἐγὼ θείοιο λαθοίμην

(My child, what sort of word escaped your teeth's barrier?
How could I forget Odysseus the godlike. . . .)

The juxtaposition of the words Ὀδυσῆος ἐγώ (Odysseus I) in
line 65 suggests hyperbole, i.e., "Me!? Forget Odysseus?!"
Zeus then points out what Athena has conveniently omitted,
namely that Odysseus is hardly an innocent victim, but has
earned Poseidon's anger by blinding his son, Polyphemos
(68–70). Having won the debate, Zeus amiably agrees to plan
Odysseus' return (76–77). Athena can scarcely believe her
ears; so the gasping effect of the hiatus in line 83 seems to
suggest as she utters the magic words, "Odysseus to return
home" (νοστῆσαι Ὀδυσῆα).[2] She happily proposes that
they send Hermes to Calypso and that she go to Ithaca (81–
95). Her eagerness is deftly suggested by the fact that she
does not wait for a reply at line 96, but immediately puts on
her travelling shoes. The interplay between Zeus and Athena

[2] The occurrence of two vowels next to one another, with no consonant in
between and nothing to mitigate it, is called hiatus. Ancient Greek authors
normally avoided it, apparently because they found the combination of vowels difficult to pronounce without making a noticeable breathing sound. It
occurs sparingly and sometimes, as here, seems to be used for special effect.

in this opening encounter presents us with subtle character drawing and serves notice to the audience that they must be sensitive at all times not only to what is said, but to how it is said; that, as in a drama, the interchange between characters is all-important. It is this aspect of the *Odyssey* more than any other which gives it its particular richness.[3]

Athena's journey shifts the scene to Ithaca, where it remains for the rest of the book. Homer's narrative art is here at its best. We expect Athena to do something and, since Hermes is to see to Odysseus' return from Calypso's island (84–87), it is natural enough that Athena should look after Odysseus' interests at home in preparation for his return there. Still, we should not miss the fact that Homer now puts the main story of Odysseus on hold to present his son and the situation on Ithaca.

Athena arrives disguised as Mentes to find the suitors preparing for dinner (106–12). She takes along a battle spear, which Homer emphasizes (99–101).

εἵλετο δ᾽ ἄλκιμον ἔγχος, ἀκαχμένον ὀξέϊ χαλκῷ,
βριθὺ μέγα στιβαρόν, τῷ δάμνησι στίχας ἀνδρῶν
ἡρώων, τοῖσίν τε κοτέσσεται ὀβριμοπάτρη.

(Then she caught up a powerful spear, edged with sharp bronze,
heavy, huge, thick, wherewith she beats down the battalions of
    fighting
men, against whom she of the mighty father is angered.)

This spear suggests the attitude with which she approaches the suitors. They, in turn, are immediately characterized in negative terms by the fact that they loll around "on the hides of cattle which they had killed" (108). To an ancient audience, for whom the consumption of meat, especially beef,

---

[3] Clay calls attention to this feature of Homer's narrative technique; see *The Wrath of Athena*, 188–90. See also, on character drawing in Homer, Griffin, *Homer on Life and Death*, 50–80, esp. 56–65. It is a well-known fact that direct speech, one character talking to another, composes more than fifty percent of the lines in this poem and in the *Iliad*.

came on rare occasions, the suitors' extravagance would be clear. Homer here introduces a theme that will be developed at length in the poem, namely eating and drinking as a touchstone of behavior. As here, eating and drinking are normally combined with the proper reception and entertaining of guests. In ancient times, as is still true in modern Greece, it was customary first to offer food and drink to a guest before asking him who he is, where he hails from, and so forth. The suitors reveal themselves throughout this first scene as totally wanting in these matters and thus as thoroughly bad.

Homer introduces Telemachus beginning at line 113. He is sitting among the suitors, daydreaming about his father returning to rid the house of them. Suddenly he catches sight of Athena/Mentes standing in the doorway and is embarrassed that a guest should be kept waiting for so long (120). These few lines brilliantly develop the situation. We have the impression that Telemachus regularly, despite his wish to be rid of them, eats with the suitors. His embarrassment suggests that for the first time he feels a responsibility as host and, more to the point, that for the first time he sees the suitors for what they are. His association with them has almost made him neglect a guest, and he now separates himself and his guest from them (132–33). Athena/Mentes reinforces his newly realized perception of the suitors when she comments on their shameless feasting (225–29). Telemachus has begun to come of age.

He is, however, a very disheartened young man who believes his father is dead (161–68) and feels sorry for himself (217–20). Athena's purpose in her interview with him is to get him moving. She does this by talking with Telemachus about his problems and offering detailed advice. Since we learn specifically at lines 189–90 that his grandfather no longer comes to the palace, we realize that this is the first serious talk he has experienced with an adult male in years. His father, after all, left for Troy when he was a baby. To Telemachus' initial statement that his father is dead (158ff.),

Athena responds that he is alive (196), predicts his return, and, under the guise of asking him if he is Odysseus' son, notes in complimentary terms that he looks like his father (208–9). Telemachus responds, "My mother says so, but I would rather have been the son of some fortunate man" (215–19). This is an extraordinary denial of his paternity. Athena brushes it aside with a curt statement that the gods have not made his lineage nameless (222–23) and changes the subject to ask about the feast. She notes that any "sensible" man (πινυτός, 229) would be outraged at these men. The implication is clear: "stop feeling sorry for yourself and do something about them," i.e., live up to your epithet "thoughtful" (πεπνυμένος).[4] Telemachus again, almost like a broken record, talks about his father's death (234–44) and describes the suitors as destroying him by eating up his substance. Athena angrily wishes that Odysseus were present to act. She then gives an account of her first encounter with Odysseus; it is a curious story and clearly made up for this moment. He was on a quest for a man-killing poison to smear on his arrows (260–64). This detail both expresses Athena's anger at the situation and conveys obliquely to Telemachus the way to deal with such men. She next tells him at length (270–96) what to do, specifically calling for the murder of the suitors (295–96), and ends by reminding him that as a grown man he should seek *kleos* such as Orestes obtained by killing his father's murderer (297–302). *Kleos* ("fame on the lips of men") is the goal par excellence of heroes;[5] her challenge to Telemachus to be a hero like his father is crystal clear. Telemachus cannot fail to understand the explicit advice; to suggest that he has understood things on a more subtle level, Homer

---

[4] Note that the words πινυτός ("sensible") and πεπνυμένος ("thoughtful") are cognate in Greek, coming from the same stem and having closely related meanings. The juxtaposition of these two words in successive lines, 229 and 230, is meaningful.

[5] For a discussion of the meaning of *kleos*, see Redfield, *Nature and Culture in the "Iliad,"* 31–33, and Nagy, *The Best of the Achaeans,* 16.

makes him comment that Mentes has spoken with kind intention "like a father to his own son" (308). Odysseus, in short, has become a great deal more real to him through this encounter (321–22).

After Athena's departure, Telemachus acts decisively towards his mother and the suitors. These scenes reinforce our sense of his growing maturity. At the same time, they give us our first impression of these important characters. Penelope, heartsick at the absence of Odysseus, comes down from her chamber to ask the singer to sing something else and not "the return" (337ff.). Telemachus, now naming his father for the first time (354)—an emblem of Odysseus' emerging reality for him—sends her back upstairs to do woman's work and asserts his power in the household (359). Penelope goes back into the house in amazement (360). Without more ado (368ff.), Telemachus turns to the suitors and tells them that tomorrow he is going to order them out of his house. The suitors, like Penelope, react with wonder (382). Antinoos points out with sneering mockery that Telemachus has spoken so boldly that he fears lest he become king, his right by birth (384–87). The audacity of a pretender to say this to the rightful heir is apparent. In the same vein, the other ringleader of the suitors, Eurymachos, wishes that Telemachus might keep his possessions. The not very veiled threat of this line, line 402, is conveyed admirably in the Greek by the hissing sound of the sigmas.[6] He then asks after the stranger and whether there is news of Odysseus' return (405–8). Telemachus, in what is very Odysseus-like behavior, carefully lies to Eurymachos (412–19), saying that his father's homecoming is lost and that the stranger claimed to be Mentes. Homer underlines the lie by his comment in line 420 that Telemachus knew in his heart that she was a goddess.

[6] The line has eight. The main verbs, which end in sigmas, are emphasized further by the fact that they are placed so as to create an internal rhyme.

The book closes with Eurykleia, the devoted nurse, putting Telemachus to bed (425–44). Having strongly portrayed rapid growth in Telemachus, Homer draws it back somewhat with this scene, which characterizes him as a child. He still has much maturing to do; the apron strings remain firmly attached in Ithaca.

This first book introduces adroitly most of the major figures and themes of the poem: Zeus, Athena, Poseidon, Polyphemos, Hermes, Calypso, Odysseus, Telemachus, Laertes, Penelope, Antinoos, Eurymachos, and Eurykleia; the accountability of men for their actions; eating and drinking/entertainment of guests as indicators of character; the story of Orestes/Agamemnon as paradigm; the journey; the use of disguise; fathers and sons. The effectiveness of this beginning is clear. It casts a wide net, while moving on the narrative level from large to small, from the council of Zeus on Olympos to the bedroom of Telemachus in Ithaca.

B O O K   T W O

The purpose of the second book is to widen the scope of the action to include the body politic of Ithaca. What had been in the first book simply a private matter between the family of Odysseus and the suitors now becomes, thanks to Telemachus' initiative, an issue for the community. The book opens with Telemachus summoning the assembly, the first one, we soon learn (26–27), since Odysseus left for Troy. Telemachus takes his father's seat amidst the elders (14). Odysseus' place is clearly an honored one at the front, among what in later parlance would be called the *proedroi*.[7] As a young man, scarcely twenty years old, Telemachus does not really have any claim on this seat other than as his father's son. These

---

[7] The seats in front reserved for the leaders of the meetings of the assembly were called by this name in Athens, for example.

actions powerfully underline his growth and depict him as-
suming his father's authority. Significantly, the elders of the
community yield to him. In this context the suitors have no
say, for as young men they have no control over the seats of
the elders; most of them in fact are not Ithacans and presumably have no right to speak at the assembly.

The poet carefully portrays a formal meeting. One of the
elders speaks first to open the meeting. The scepter, the emblem of authority, is held by Telemachus as he speaks (38).
This setting allows the poet to depict the suitors shamelessly
admitting their murderous intentions towards Odysseus and
his house in front of the legally constituted assembly of Ithacans. Confident in their numbers, the suitors have no regard for anyone.

The assembly (1–259) falls into two parts (39–145, 157–256).
The omen of the eagles marks the dividing point. In the first
part Telemachus addresses the Ithacans and makes a public
complaint against the suitors. Antinoos, their leader, brazenly admits the truth of Telemachus' accusations and
blames everything on Penelope. He even has the temerity to
suggest that Telemachus send his mother home to her father.
Telemachus dismisses this suggestion and (in good debating
fashion) turns it back on Antinoos, telling him to get out. He
ends by saying that, if they do not go, he will call on the gods
to grant a reversal so that the suitors might perish in his
house unavenged. Telemachus here is clearly going on public
record; he knows the suitors too well to think that they will
depart. As any good bargainer will do, he begins with his
most extreme position. In the second part he introduces his
real demand of the suitors, namely that they grant him a ship
to go in search of news of his father (212–15). In their disdain
for Telemachus, the suitors with Leokritos as their spokesman sarcastically suggest that Mentor and Halitherses ar-
range for Telemachus' journey! The implication is that they
either will not dare or will not be able to do it. The suitors

here exhibit the overconfidence that will eventually prove their downfall.

Telemachus' request for a ship is a very reasonable one, for his journey promises to end the deadlock. Since they all believe Odysseus to be dead, the suitors should favor his mission. Homer, therefore, carefully arranges the narrative so that when Telemachus' proposal comes the suitors are in no mood for cooperation. The omen of the eagles (146–54) and Halitherses' reading of it (161–76) precede. There is no obvious relationship between two eagles fighting above the assembly and the interpretation made of it, namely that it portends the return of Odysseus and the death of the suitors.[8] Rather, the appearance of the birds seems an excuse for Halitherses to address the assembly, predict death for the suitors, and call upon his fellow citizens to restrain them (168). The suitors are naturally put on the defensive and their spokesman, Eurymachos, threatens their accuser (178ff.). Immediately following Telemachus' request, Mentor, another elder, speaks (225ff.), again pointing out the outrageous acts of the suitors against the house of Odysseus (236–38), and calling upon the Ithacans to restrain them (241). Stung by the continued attack, the suitors via their spokesman Leokritos (243ff.) do not reply directly to Telemachus, but rather rebut Mentor, dare the Ithacans to try, and derisively suggest that Mentor and Halitherses help Telemachus (253–54).

Homer artfully aligns Telemachus with the elders, i.e., those who represent the community. Not only does he sit with them, but he, Halitherses, and Mentor address their remarks first and foremost to the Ithacans, that is, to the assembly and to the wider community (65ff., 161, 229). In fact, when Telemachus deigns to make his direct request for help to the suitors (209–12), Mentor, as if in correction of his tactical error, redirects the debate to the Ithacans and the con-

[8] For brief comments on this omen, see Podlecki, "Omens in the *Odyssey*," 17–18.

duct of the suitors (229–41). The three spokesmen for the suitors, Antinoos, Eurymachos, and Leokritos, each show their viciousness a little more clearly as the assembly progresses. Antinoos admits Telemachus' accusations and cheekily tells him how to handle his mother. Eurymachos, in response to Halitherses, resorts to crude threats of physical violence (179, 183, 190, 192) and sarcasm (200) directed not just at Halitherses, but above all at Telemachus. Leokritos (243–56) openly articulates the suitors' trust in their numbers and makes it clear that they have no intention of yielding to Odysseus should he return. His is a remarkable statement of lawlessness; they will not give way even to the rightful king (246–51). Leokritos here earns the death that he receives at Telemachus' hands in book twenty-two.

The speech of Antinoos (85–128) gives us an important new perspective on Penelope. In the first book she had been merely a foil against which to show the growing independence of a son. Here in a context where he means to cast blame, Antinoos cannot help showing his admiration for Penelope's cleverness. Homer suggests this in part by his use of an incomplete sentence at lines 115–122—the if-clause of line 115 has no answering main clause. This faulty syntax, known technically as an anacoluthon, comes just at the point where Antinoos praises Penelope in spite of himself. It mirrors on the syntactic level his mental confusion. It is also in this speech that we hear for the first time of the stratagem of the web (94–110), the very hallmark of Penelope's resourcefulness. Her demure act of weaving a shroud for the eldest male of her family constituted a wifely duty that even the suitors had to respect. She has used it to stall the suitors for more than three years. Despite his annoyance, Antinoos' emphasis on the length of time ("much time," πολὺν χρόνον in line 115) suggests that this stratagem is what has provoked his admiration. This sets the groundwork for the poet's vivid presentation of Penelope in the second half of the poem.

The aftermath of the assembly forms the second major section of book two (260–434). It begins piquantly (259–60):

μνηστῆρες δ᾽ ἐς δώματ᾽ ἴσαν θείου Ὀδυσῆος.
Τηλέμαχος δ᾽ ἀπάνευθε κιὼν ἐπὶ θῖνα θαλάσσης

(The suitors proceeded into the home of godly Odysseus.
Telemachus going apart along the strand of the sea. . . .)

(My trans.)

The juxtaposition of proper names, Odysseus at the end of one line and Telemachus at the beginning of the next, forcefully underlines what is wrong in Ithaca. Telemachus' prayer by the sea nicely recalls Achilles' prayer to his mother by the sea strand in *Iliad* 1.350. The reminiscence enhances Telemachus' stature and does much to give us a sense of his true anger and frustration.[9] Now, having made his case public, Telemachus sets about planning his journey. Each of his actions suggests his new-found maturity. He knows enough to pray for help to the god who visited him yesterday (262). He next spurns Antinoos, who invites him to eat and offers him a ship (305–8). The offer is a private one, the acceptance of which would place Telemachus intolerably in Antinoos' debt. He then proceeds to the storerooms to secure provisions from Eurykleia (337ff.). Carefully reinforcing our view of the suitors, the poet portrays the old nurse as thinking that they plan to kill Telemachus (367–68). She therefore attempts to restrain him, but he brushes aside her fears and swears her to an oath of silence (373ff.). Telemachus here moves out from the influence of the suitors and the women of his household and now comes under Athena's tutelage. Homer stresses Athena's controlling role (382, 393, 405) and Telemachus' dependence on her (406, 416–17). As the book had begun with Telemachus on his way to the assembly, it closes

[9] Homer has prepared for this by Telemachus' dramatic gesture of throwing down the scepter at line 80; this act recalls Achilles' far more symbolic gesture in the opening scenes of the *Iliad*.

with him on shipboard, accompanied by Athena and headed toward Pylos. Each of these journeys marks a significant step in his coming of age.

BOOK THREE

Telemachus arrives at Pylos and is welcomed cordially by Nestor. He soon discovers that Nestor has no news of his father. Why, one may ask, does Homer, on a journey the specific purpose of which is to gain news of Odysseus, have Telemachus go to someone who can give him no news and in fact has not seen or heard of his father since the day they left Troy ten years ago? Clearly Telemachus' journey encompasses more than the mere acquisition of news. The journey is one of growth and learning for Telemachus, learning not only about his father but also about proper modes of behavior. There is no better person to serve as his first host and teacher than Nestor, the senior statesman among those who were at Troy with his father. Nestor represents in the flesh the world and values of Telemachus' father.

Nestor and his sons teach Telemachus proper behavior in word and in deed. The time Telemachus spends with Nestor (i.e., book three) takes place almost entirely at sacrifices, first to Poseidon (1–341) and then to Athena (380–473). The contrast between these ceremonies at Pylos and the goings-on in Ithaca at Odysseus' palace could not be greater. Telemachus needs role models other than the suitors; Nestor and his family provide the initial one. Performing sacrifices at the proper time and in the correct manner was extremely important for the well-being of states and individuals in the ancient world. Telemachus here learns by doing. Note also how well the poet intertwines the themes of his poem by having Telemachus honor the two gods who are most interested in his father, the one for him, the other against. His sacrifice to Poseidon looks ahead to the eventual homage that Odysseus must pay to Poseidon in order to make peace with him (11.120–36). The honor Telemachus pays to Athena underlines the special relationship that he and his father share with Athena. This shared relationship soon becomes a powerful indicator of their fundamental similarity. A didactic tone permeates the book. Telemachus has come from a very bad situation at home. We the audience know it and so we do not find it inappropriate that everyone at Pylos sets an example for him or gives him explicit advice. Athena disguised as Mentor literally guides him as the book opens. Note the emphatic repetition of her name combined with the idea of leading in lines 12–13.

ἐκ δ᾿ ἄρα Τηλέμαχος νηὸς βαῖν᾿, ἄρχε δ᾿ ᾿Αθήνη.
τὸν προτέρη προσέειπε θεὰ γλαυκῶπις ᾿Αθήνη·

(Telemachus stepped out of the ship, but Athena went first, and it was the gray-eyed goddess Athena who first spoke to him.)

After reassuring Telemachus, who is diffident about approaching Nestor, "Pallas Athena led the way swiftly; he followed along in the footsteps of the goddess" (29–30). The physical action represents clearly his dependence on her. Athena/Mentor prays to Poseidon (55–61). Instead of giving Telemachus a separate prayer, the poet depicts his continuing dependence by saying merely that he prayed "in the same way" as Athena (64). And, before Telemachus speaks for the first time, she puts courage into him (76).

Nestor and his son Peisistratos also instruct Telemachus. Artfully mirroring the story pattern that he has chosen, Homer shows us the son before the father. Peisistratos comes forward to greet the guests, seats them, gives them food, and then addresses them (36–50). Here he fulfills the role of dutiful son by acting on behalf of his father. Although he is Telemachus' age, he acts with complete self-assurance. In short, Peisistratos provides by his example a paradigm for Telemachus, and at lines 49–50 he offers the initial lesson in etiquette, explaining that deference is owed first to the older person.

It is Nestor who proves to be the chief teacher of Telemachus in this book. As Peisistratos plays the archetypal son, so Nestor becomes the father. He puts into words several important lessons. At lines 69–70 he enunciates the most important element in the proper treatment of guests, namely that they should be fed first and questioned later. He observes sagely that "the anger of the gods is not suddenly turned" (147). Though given to Telemachus, the lesson is really more suited to Odysseus and is indicative of the blending of the roles of father and son that runs throughout the poem. Most obviously, Nestor ends his two long speeches to Telemachus (103–200, 254–328) by pointing out a particular moral, namely that like Orestes, Telemachus should be a true son of his father (196–200), and that he should not stay away from home too long lest, like Menelaos, he return home to find destruction in his house (313–16). Lastly, it is Nestor who specifically advises him to visit Menelaos (317–28) and explains to him that Athena has been his companion (377–79).

Apart from these specific lessons, Nestor has the more important function of putting Telemachus in direct contact for the first time with his father's world. After the boorishness of the suitors, the courtly Nestor opens the young man's eyes. From Nestor he hears of the departure from Troy, learns of his father's prowess as a speaker, and, at lines 124–29, receives Nestor's astonished admiration for speaking just like his father. He also learns that Athena had particular concern for his father at Troy from Nestor's wish that she would also love Telemachus and help him against the suitors (218–24). Above all, Nestor tells him at some length (193–200, 254–312), but at second hand, about Agamemnon's return. The story's significance for Telemachus is stressed not just as an example, but also because meeting someone who possesses more direct information will bring his own experience of his father's world nearly up to date. Nestor's firsthand knowledge stopped very shortly after the departure from Troy (180–84), and so Telemachus must journey on to Sparta to see Menelaos.

To all this teaching Telemachus proves an apt pupil. His first speech (79–101) does not occur until he has observed Peisistratos, heard Nestor's first and most important lesson in etiquette (69–70), and been encouraged by Athena (76). In tone it is excessively pessimistic. He is a very discouraged young man after all, and he has made up his mind that his father is dead. He simply wants to know the details. Words for death and dying dominate in lines 87–95 and reveal his negative frame of mind. He must shed this pessimism to grow. In style, however, his speech is wholly admirable. The sonorous, full address of his opening line, "Nestor, sprung of Neleus, shining honor of the Achaians," shows proper deference. The three lines that follow contrast effectively; the clauses are short, the ideas self-contained. Each line expresses one or more complete ideas and ends with a period. Telemachus wastes no time in getting to the point. As he speaks of his father, he warms to his subject and gains in confidence. The style reveals this by broadening out, for the next nine lines (83–91) fall into three periodic sentences of three lines each. Telemachus begins his final section with an emotional plea to Nestor to tell him about his father's death. Style again effectively reinforces meaning; here for the first four lines (92–95), instead of sense units coinciding with verse end, as is normal in Homeric verse and up to this point regular practice in this speech, the sense runs over from one line to the next for three successive verses. This device is called enjambment and is clearly meant to express Telemachus' strong feelings. He ends his speech as he had begun by naming his father and appealing to Nestor's and Odysseus' common experience at Troy. It is a polished piece and Nestor believably praises it (124–25).

Nestor ends his reply to this speech by hinting that he has detailed knowledge of Agamemnon's return and murder about which Telemachus might well be curious (193–95). He obviously invites a follow-up. Telemachus does not take the hint, for he is too busy feeling sorry for himself and his father (208–9). Nestor tries to encourage him by pointing out that Athena has aided his father in the past and may well help him too against the suitors. Telemachus refuses to be encouraged and in his pessimism utters what amounts to blasphemy (226–28):

ὦ γέρον, οὔ πω τοῦτο ἔπος τελέεσθαι ὀΐω·
λίην γὰρ μέγα εἶπες· ἄγη μ' ἔχει. οὐκ ἂν ἐμοί γε
ἐλπομένῳ τὰ γένοιτ', οὐδ' εἰ θεοὶ ὣς ἐθέλοιεν.

(Old sir, I think what you have said will not be accomplished.
What you mean is too big. It bewilders me. That which I hope
for
could never happen to me, not even if the gods so willed it.)

Athena/Mentor corrects him vigorously, claiming without qualification that "a god, if he so wishes it, could easily save a man even from afar" (231). Her next words, "I could wish," lead us for a moment to think that she has forgotten her disguise. She quickly catches herself and uses of herself words that really apply to Odysseus in order to turn the subject back to Agamemnon (232–34).

βουλοίμην δ' ἂν ἐγώ γε καὶ ἄλγεα πολλὰ μογήσας
οἴκαδέ τ' ἐλθέμεναι καὶ νόστιμον ἦμαρ ἰδέσθαι,
ἢ ἐλθὼν ἀπολέσθαι ἐφέστιος, ὡς Ἀγαμέμνων

(I myself would rather first have gone through many hardships
and then come home, and look upon my day of returning,
than come home and be killed at my own hearth, as
Agamemnon. . . .)

Athena really implies here more than Mentor can know about Odysseus, but covers it up by seeming to admit his death in the next breath (236–38).

ἀλλ᾽ ἦ τοι θάνατον μὲν ὁμοίϊον οὐδὲ θεοί περ
καὶ φίλῳ ἀνδρὶ δύνανται ἀλαλκέμεν, ὁππότε κεν δὴ
μοῖρ᾽ ὀλοὴ καθέλῃσι τανηλεγέος θανάτοιο.

(But death is a thing that comes to all alike. Not even
the gods can fend it away from a man they love, when once
the destructive doom of leveling death has fastened upon him.)

This is a remarkably effective speech, for it provokes Telemachus to respond and prompts him to follow up on Nestor's hint. He speaks first to Mentor and dismisses talk of Odysseus' homecoming. Then he turns to Nestor to ask details of Agamemnon's death and especially the whereabouts of Menelaos. His tone is assertive towards Athena/Mentor and suggests a growing independence, while towards Nestor he shows great deference, even reverence, on account of his age (244–46). His questions reveal him wanting to learn, to imbibe more of the story that has been held up to him as an example.

Nestor now fully takes on the role of guide (317–28) and Athena takes her departure (371). Telemachus, in being told that his companion was Athena, now must know in fact that he is favored by her as his father is. His growth and newfound grace are symbolized by the bath that he is given while the sacrifice to Athena is being prepared. He emerges from the bath "looking like an immortal" (468) to take part in the feast. This bath marks the completion of the first stage of his journey. He is ready to continue on to Lacedaemon, but now, instead of Athena/Mentor, young Peisistratos serves as guide and confidante. Telemachus has learned much about himself; he also has a clearer perception of his father and his father's world than he has ever had. Athena/Mentor, Peisistratos, and Nestor have taught him well. The raucous behavior of the suitors on the one hand and the apron strings of his mother and Eurykleia on the other have receded far into the background as he drives off toward Sparta.

BOOK FOUR

Book four falls into three parts of roughly equal length. In the first (1–305) Telemachus and Peisistratos are welcomed by Menelaos and Helen; memories of the Trojan War and Odysseus' actions predominate. The central section (306–624) gives us the meeting between Menelaos and Telemachus and the story of Proteus. It also brings the wanderings of Odysseus and Menelaos up to date and predicts the future. The third section (625–847) gives us the current situation on Ithaca, namely the reactions of the suitors and Penelope to the news of Telemachus' journey.

Book four completes Telemachus' education. At Pylos he participated in sacrifices; now in Sparta he takes part in another very serious occasion of eating and drinking, one that symbolizes the stability and continuity of family life, namely a wedding feast. The emphasis is on the milieu of family, the hero *en famille* as it were. Telemachus again experiences what is his father's goal. Homer also keeps the motif of showing proper hospitality to guests at the fore by having Menelaos very near the beginning of the book rebuke his companion Eteoneus for wondering whether to invite the strangers in (31ff.). The ethos of the etiquette lesson continues.

At the opening of the book Telemachus appears somewhat inexperienced and gauche. Overawed by the splendor of Menelaos' palace (43ff.), he blurts out his wonder to Peisistratos (71–75). By the end of his stay, he meets privately with Menelaos (Peisistratos' absence marks his growth) and can tactfully suggest that Menelaos' parting gift of horses and chariot will hardly be of use on rugged Ithaca (600–608). Far from being put off, Menelaos is amused and offers another more appropriate gift, a silver and gold mixing bowl. It is a king's gift (618) and fit for one. Telemachus has completed his education and become the royal son of a royal father. As a further emblem of this coming of age, he is thrice (21, 303, 312) in this book styled "hero" (ἥρως). Homer portrays this growth in several ways. Above all, Telemachus gains a much better knowledge of his father, who he is and who he was. Without this knowledge, he cannot become like his father. First he learns from Helen's immediate recognition of him (140ff.) that he bears an uncanny resemblance to his father, both in physique and in mien (149–50). He then hears of his father's exploits in the final days of Troy—exploits that emphasize Odysseus' cleverness and superior leadership (235–89). Helen's tale of his entering Troy in disguise prefigures what Odysseus will do on his return to Ithaca; Menelaos' choice of an incident connected with the wooden horse pointedly brings before Telemachus his father's most famous stratagem. Finally and most importantly, throughout this book Telemachus associates with Menelaos, a man who feels an especial kinship with Odysseus (105ff., 171ff.), perhaps because his experiences have been so similar to those of Odysseus.[10] After wandering much and suffering much (81, 95: these are phrases used of Odysseus in the proem), Menelaos has returned in the eighteenth year. He has had to overcome a sea god (Proteus) to do it. Along the way he was becalmed on an island and aided by a goddess, Eidothea (360–67). These careful correspondences with Odysseus' adventures are intended, I think, to suggest that Telemachus is getting real experience of his father by being with Menelaos. Menelaos, in short, becomes a surrogate father. Telemachus' new-found experience of his father receives its finishing touch from Proteus' report (555–60) that

---

[10] On the similarities, see also J. H. Finley, Homer's "Odyssey," 149–54, and Anderson, "Calypso and Elysium."

Odysseus is not dead, but is detained by Calypso. Now Telemachus can have real hope of actually seeing his father
alive.

In contrast to Nestor, who draws explicit lessons for Telemachus at the end of each of his speeches, Menelaos presents
paradigms of behavior and leaves it to Telemachus to draw
the conclusions. His own return implies the return of Odysseus, while the subduing of Proteus by tenaciously hanging
on surely suggests to Telemachus that he should persevere.
Above all, Menelaos' reaction at the beginning of their interview on learning of the behavior of the suitors (333–46) expresses an heroic faith in Odysseus' return. He employs a
simile (335–40) comparing Odysseus to a lion and the suitors
to fawns and prays to the gods for Odysseus' return and vengeance. This simile is the first extended one in the poem and,
quite unusually, it occurs in direct speech. The tone is lofty;
Menelaos here, as king, speaks with great solemnity.[11]

In addition to these more or less explicit lessons, Homer
creates at the court of Menelaos an uneasy ambience that requires from the two young men developed social skills. Peisistratos handles the first situation and provides, as part of
Telemachus' learning experience, an exemplum. He reminds
them all at lines 190 and following that there is a time for
weeping and it is surely not just as you have set a meal for
guests. Somehow Helen and Menelaos get carried away. In
any case, they have a tense home situation that requires vig-
ilance on the part of a guest lest he become embroiled in it.
Helen, after all, is the root cause of their sufferings, sufferings that cannot fully be dispelled, even by her drugs (220).
The byplay between Helen and Menelaos as they recount the
deeds of Odysseus (235ff.) brings the tension between them

---

[11] Near the close of the book there is another extended lion simile, this
time of Penelope as she frets about the suitors' plan to kill Telemachus (791–
93). The parallel between Odysseus and Penelope is notable. The lion simile
again of Odysseus in the sixth book (130–35) reinforces the impression that
Homer restricts this animal comparison to the royal family.

out into the open.[12] Helen's story puts her own actions in the best possible light. She did not betray Odysseus, even though she recognized him, and she rejoiced at the deaths of the Trojans because by then she had experienced a change of heart (260) and wanted to go home. In any case Aphrodite caused it all (261–62). Menelaos does not say "blast your lying eyes"; rather, his story (266ff.) puts the lie to her. It is set on Troy's final night, i.e., after the reputed time of Helen's tale. Helen, as she comes to the horse, is accompanied by Deiphobos (276)—Menelaos does not need to add "your husband after Paris"—and tries to trick the Greeks into giving themselves away. Of course, he adds, a god made you do it (274–75). Only an anesthetized hearer will fail to perceive that a quarrel between host and hostess is imminent. Telemachus, who has said nothing since his whispered words to Peisistratos (71ff.), now takes charge (291–95) and forestalls any further awkwardness:

Ἀτρεΐδη Μενέλαε διοτρεφές, ὄρχαμε λαῶν,
ἄλγιον· οὐ γάρ οἵ τι τάδ᾽ ἤρκεσε λυγρὸν ὄλεθρον,
οὐδ᾽ εἰ οἱ κραδίη γε σιδηρέη ἔνδοθεν ἦεν.
ἀλλ᾽ ἄγετ᾽ εἰς εὐνὴν τράπεθ᾽ ἡμέας, ὄφρα καὶ ἤδη
ὕπνῳ ὕπο γλυκερῷ ταρπώμεθα κοιμηθέντες.

(Great Menelaos, son of Atreus, leader of the people:
so much the worse; for none of all this kept dismal destruction
from him [Odysseus], not even if he had a heart of iron within
    him.
But come, take us away to our beds, so that at last now
we can go to bed and enjoy the pleasure of sweet sleep.)

So the evening ends with this reminder of Odysseus from Telemachus. He has gained a good deal of self-assurance to intervene at such a delicate moment and is clearly ready to proceed on his own, which he does on the next day in the

[12] See also on this incident Beye, The "Iliad," the "Odyssey" and the Epic Tradition, 173–74.

tête-à-tête with Menelaos. It is notable in the structure of the book that this action completes section one, and his adroit handling of Menelaos' guest gift (600–619) brings the second part to a close. Homer thus emphasizes structurally Telemachus' maturation.

Homer will introduce Odysseus on Calypso's island in the next book. He thus devotes the final section of this book (625–847) to developing the situation on Ithaca so as to juxtapose Ithaca/Penelope and the initial appearance of Odysseus. The primary purpose of this section is to set before us, before we leave them for nine books, the suitors and their utter depravity. At lines 663 and following they plan, at Antinoos' suggestion, to murder Telemachus on the pretext that he has gone against their wishes. To underscore the enormity of the situation, Homer immediately shows us Penelope's heartbroken reaction (675–766, esp. 703–5). The book closes with a description of the suitors preparing the ambush (778–86, 842–47); these lines nicely frame a scene in which Penelope is reassured in a dream that Athena will safeguard her son. The poet deliberately eschews suspense in order to show the suitors as depraved and acting to no purpose.

CHAPTER 2

Books Five to Eight

BOOKS FIVE TO EIGHT introduce us to Odysseus on Calypso's island. The poet at the outset has placed his hero in a most dangerous situation, for human lovers of goddesses routinely pay the ultimate price for their presumption. Moreover, when we first see Odysseus, he has already rejected Calypso and her offer of immortality. His commitment to being a man, not a god, is thereby emphatically underlined, and his death would be imminent if it were not for Hermes' intervention. Men suffer and die; the end of life's journey is death. Odysseus' journeys become metaphors for this fact. They are more elemental than his son's and involve symbolic deaths and rebirths. The first of these journeys in book five from Calypso ("the burier") through Leukothea ("the white goddess") to Phaeacia establishes this symbolic meaning for all of Odysseus' journeys. Books six to eight then depict the "reborn" Odysseus having the experiences of a young man; he meets a young woman, goes home to meet her parents, and wins her hand. This motif of rebirth and growth confers upon this tetrad a strong unity. As a device for both suggesting Odysseus' youth and reminding us of his own family on Ithaca, Homer includes a number of parallels between Odysseus' experiences among the Phaeacians and Telemachus' in Pylos and at Sparta. Eating and drinking and treatment of guests also continue to play a prominent role, in both Calypso's reception of Hermes and the Phaeacians' of Odysseus.

Often the interlude on Phaeacia is perceived as a time of peaceful rest for Odysseus, a kind of halfway house to Ithaca. One will appreciate these books best, however, if one sees that they constitute a "dry run" in preparation for Ithaca and challenge Odysseus to the utmost.[1] He finds himself here in a very delicate, not to say dangerous, position. He becomes involved with the daughter of a king whose help he desperately needs. In initially gaining the goodwill of the princess, he plays on her inevitable inclinations for marriage and succeeds too well. She falls for him. He must now win the favor of her parents, who know their daughter's mind, without giving away too soon his identity, lest her parents think that he, a married man, has been toying with their daughter's affections. These books show Odysseus at his most adroit in deception and in using what he has, namely words, to gain what he needs.

BOOK FIVE

In book five we encounter Odysseus in person for the first time. The book therefore has particular emphasis, and the poet sets it apart in large and in small. The first two lines, for example, describe day dawning, a common enough occurrence in the poem.

Ἠὼς δ᾽ ἐκ λεχέων παρ᾽ ἀγαυοῦ Τιθωνοῖο
ὄρνυθ᾽, ἵν᾽ ἀθανάτοισι φόως φέροι ἠδὲ βροτοῖσιν·

(Now Dawn rose from her bed, where she lay by haughty
Tithonos,
carrying light to the immortal gods and to mortals.)

What is not common is that these particular lines occur only here in the *Odyssey*, as though to emphasize the new beginning. Dawn, the first word in the Greek, provides a strong, not to say abrupt, opening. In subject matter the book covers one complete action, the journey of Odysseus from Calypso's island to the land of the Phaeacians. It makes a satisfying, nearly self-contained, unit, which opens with the gods on

[1] On the ambiguous character of the Phaeacians, see Clarke, *The Art of the "Odyssey,"* 52–54.

Olympos and closes with the hero asleep on Phaeacia (as, incidentally, book one opened with the gods and closed with Telemachus tucked in bed on Ithaca). The quiet of the close contrasts very effectively with the tumult of the storm that precedes it. Odysseus' resourcefulness in building the raft, his courage in the face of the elements, his state of exhaustion at the close stand out against the sweeping backdrop of the sea and the divine machinery. He is, significantly, the only mortal in the book; he is the focus of all action and his stature is magnified by it. It is a tremendous, if somewhat surprising, introduction to our hero.

Much has been written in criticism of the second council of the gods with which the book opens, on the grounds that it is an unnecessary and inartistic repetition of the council at the opening of book one. Such criticism misses the fact that the second council is a conscious doublet with a clear purpose. These critics have failed to appreciate just how successfully the poet has recreated the council, at the same time avoiding almost completely the repetition of lines from the first council (1.26–95). Only lines 21–22 (= 1.63–64) and 30–31 (= 1.86–87) come from the first council. In a style where repetition not only is *not* avoided, but is used freely—and there are significant repetitions in these lines (8–12 = 2.230–34, 14–17 = 4.557–60, 19–20 = 4.701–2)—the avoidance of lines in the second council from the first seems a deliberate device to emphasize the new mission, which focuses on Odysseus. In short, the second council has been carefully composed for this spot. It is the poet's way of taking us back to the beginning and indicating a rough simultaneity of action between Telemachus' adventures in books one to four and his father's in books five to eight. Since the poet must necessarily tell his story sequentially, he can, so to speak, "have his cake and eat it too." That is, while having the approximate simultaneity of Athena's and Hermes' missions, he can also make Athena refer for rhetorical reasons to the suitors' plan to kill Telemachus at the end of book four.

Except for the council of the gods and Hermes' journey (1–54), the book falls almost into halves: lines 55–268 are set at Calypso's island; lines 269–493 recount the departure from Calypso, the storm, and the arrival at Phaeacia. Calypso enlivens the first half. She has a quick temper. At lines 87 and following, sensing the purpose of Hermes' visit, she peremptorily questions him before remembering her manners and offering food and drink (91–95). This near breach of etiquette sufficiently suggests her state of mind. Note also that Hermes feels the need to remind her at lines 103–4 that it is not possible for her to flout Zeus' will. She needs the warning, for her speech (118–44) is a barely controlled piece of vitriol. She attacks the gods, particularly Zeus, and ends defiantly (140): "Send him away! no way will I!" (πέμψω δέ μιν οὔ πη ἐγώ γε). The explanatory sentences that follow (141–44), "for I have no ships, etc.," are merely a sop, as Hermes' reaction makes clear (146–47):

> οὕτω νῦν ἀπόπεμπε, Διὸς δ᾽ ἐποπίζεο μῆνιν,
> μή πώς τοι μετόπισθε κοτεσσάμενος χαλεπήνῃ.

(So send him away at once and watch out for the rage of Zeus lest angry he should treat you harshly hereafter.)   (My trans.)

Having seen Calypso's temper for ourselves, we appreciate Odysseus' wisdom later on when he exacts an oath from her that she intends him no harm (178–88).

The second half of the book, which depicts Odysseus at Poseidon's mercy, tossed about by the elements, contains an unusually high number of extended similes. There are five in the final 200 lines as compared with one or two for most books of the poem. These similes are another device that elevates this book and the poet's initial presentation of his main character. They illuminate Odysseus' helplessness before Poseidon; in all except the last, the passivity of his situation is stressed. His raft is carried hither and thither over the deep just as the spring wind blows puff balls across a field (328–30). The planks of the raft are scattered just as a gusting wind scatters a pile of dry chaff (368–70). Raised up on a wave, the sight of land appears as welcome to him as a sign of life is welcome to the children of a father who has been deathly ill (394–98). Pried loose from the rocks by the backwash of a wave, the skin is pulled from his hands just as an octopus's suckers pull stones loose from the rock when it is dragged from its lair (432–35). The final simile highlights Odysseus' last action in the book; it is an act that brings things full circle. The hero who has escaped Calypso (*Kalypsō* in Greek) now buries himself (the verb is *kalypsato*, 491) in a bed of leaves to preserve his life, just as someone far out in the country hides a brand in the ash to preserve the seed of fire (488–91). The narrowness of his escape from death at sea is thus deftly expressed.

As soon as Hermes reaches Calypso's island, we are treated to a description of a lush, tropical paradise (58–74) filled with sweet smells, sounds, and sights. Gauguin never painted a more sensual scene. With this as the context, Homer now gives us our first direct view of Odysseus who, far from basking in the joys of this paradise, sits on the beach bitterly weeping and gazing out to sea (82–84). The juxtaposition emphasizes the picture. We understand without needing to be told the meaning of Odysseus' gesture. He longs for home. His rejection of the easy life takes on even greater emphasis, for we soon learn that Calypso desired to marry him (120) and promised to make him immortal and ageless (136). How can he refuse immortality? What more could a man want? A hero, and Odysseus is a hero, needs *kleos*, fame on the lips of men, without which he is nothing. Calypso, as Hermes not very politely says, lives far out in the ocean away from the cities of men (100–102). To stay with her, therefore, represents a loss of *kleos*, namely a loss of identity and death.[2] Calypso has other important associations with death. Her very name is derived from the verb *kalyptō*, which is a common word in Greek for burying, and her island is located most strikingly "where the navel of the sea is" (1.50). For the Greeks the navel marked the entrance to the underworld, as did the famed navel stone at Delphi.

In giving his hero the option of becoming immortal, the poet has depicted as emphatically as possible Odysseus' renewed commitment to his given lot. He is a mortal, a human being, whose fate it is to die. Immortality is not for him, nor, Homeric poetry suggests, for any man. The trials and tribulations of the gods are trivial precisely because they live forever. By a harsh paradox, it is death, the fact that one will not always be alive, which makes life important. In the course of his seven-year stay with Calypso, Odysseus has found, despite the real temptation, that the idyllic round of pleasure that she offers holds no meaning. At best, it represents a vegetable existence.[3] By the time we first encounter him, therefore, he has come to reject her offer of immortality and has committed himself to living life with all its suffering to the fullest.

Homer reinforces the idea that Odysseus' stay with Calypso has been a kind of living death by casting the journey away from her island in terms that strongly suggest a rebirth. Hermes with his wand, with which he both mazes the eyes of men whom he wishes and wakes the sleeping (47–48), initiates the journey. This is Hermes guider of souls. Leukothea/Ino saves Odysseus from death in the storm. Both of her

[2] Thus in preferring *kleos* Odysseus in fact chooses the only type of immortality really open in Homeric terms to a mortal. In epic, as Nagy points out (*The Best of the Achaeans*, 148–50), the hero strives for honor that approximates that of the gods.

[3] On the living death that Calypso offers, see also Anderson, "Calypso and Elysium," 81–85.

names are symbolic: the first means "white goddess"; the second appears to be from the stem *in-*, signifying "sinew" or "strength." At the end of the journey Odysseus emerges from the sea naked and seeks refuge from the elements in an olive copse. The simile at lines 394–98 explicitly compares this journey to a return to life and also, very significantly in terms of Odysseus' final goal, places it in a family context.

ὡς δ' ὅτ' ἂν ἀσπάσιος βίοτος παίδεσσι φανήῃ
πατρός, ὃς ἐν νούσῳ κεῖται κρατέρ' ἄλγεα πάσχων,
δηρὸν τηκόμενος, στυγερὸς δέ οἱ ἔχραε δαίμων,
ἀσπάσιον δ' ἄρα τόν γε θεοὶ κακότητος ἔλυσαν,
ὣς Ὀδυσῆ' ἀσπαστὸν ἐείσατο γαῖα καὶ ὕλη

(And as welcome as the show of life again in a father
is to his children, when he has lain sick, suffering
    strong pains,
and wasting long away, and the hateful death spirit has
    brushed him,
but then, and it is welcome, the gods set him free of his
    sickness,
so welcome appeared land and forest now to Odysseus.)

The final simile of the book, the simile of preserving the spark of fire in the ash, completes the idea. The bright spark in the dark ash recalls the white goddess whose veil preserves, in contrast to the burier whose clothes must be shed to survive (372–73). The word for spark in this simile, *sperma* (490), powerfully suggests birth; it occurs only here in Homer and is a technical word, meaning "seed," that has the same connotations as "sperm" in English. With the aid of this simile Odysseus' act of burying himself (491) takes on a protective, preserving function, the opposite of the burying that Calypso threatened at the start of the book. Homer reinforces this altered image of burying by the final word of the book, *amphikalypsas*, "bury round about, bury thoroughly" (493); he now uses it to describe Athena covering Odysseus' eyes in sleep, a sleep that he desperately needs to regain his strength.

The raft-building (243–61) joins together the two halves of the book. This is the first action of any note that Odysseus takes in the poem, and it necessarily goes far to characterize him. Working with his hands, in this case constructing an elaborate raft, is not the normal activity of a hero. The description is complex and so is the craft created. The episode portrays Odysseus' skill with his hands and affirms him from the outset as the man who uses his intelligence, his cleverness to overcome the obstacles on his return home. This will be developed in the next section, books nine to twelve, as the dominant characteristic that he must cultivate in order to survive the adventures and recover his kingdom. That he knows how to construct a seaworthy vessel, sail and all, suggests his affinity with the Phaeacians, the best sailors in the poem, and anticipates his reception there.

Before leaving book five, we should take a moment to consider lines 173–79, Odysseus' first words in the poem. Let us remind ourselves of the context. Odysseus has been on Calypso's island for some seven years and long since has been yearning to get home. One day Calypso comes to him where he sits on the shore crying and "his sweet life's strength" is "slipping away"—so the unexpectedly metaphorical phrase, κατείβετο δὲ γλυκὺς αἰών (152), should be translated. Calypso now promises what he has so long yearned for, to send him on his way willingly, and advises him to build a raft. She will stock it and send a favorable wind (162–67). Far from welcoming her suggestion, "long-suffering, shining Odysseus shuddered" (ῥίγησεν δὲ πολύτλας δῖος Ὀδυσσεύς, 171). The verb "shuddered" (ῥίγησεν) occurs also at line 116 of this book, where it describes Calypso's very angry reaction to the message delivered by Hermes. Here it marks an

equally strong reaction and underscores one of the traits that
will come to characterize Odysseus in the poem, his gut instinct to trust no one. Despite the strong emotion suggested
by the verb, the words that follow depict a shrewd and controlled man (173–79).

Ἄλλο τι δὴ σύ, θεά, τόδε μήδεαι οὐδέ τι πομπήν,
ἥ με κέλεαι σχεδίῃ περάαν μέγα λαῖτμα θαλάσσης,
δεινόν τ᾽ ἀργαλέον τε· τὸ δ᾽ οὐδ᾽ ἐπὶ νῆες ἐῖσαι
ὠκύποροι περόωσιν, ἀγαλλόμεναι Διὸς οὔρῳ.
οὐδ᾽ ἂν ἐγὼν ἀέκητι σέθεν σχεδίης ἐπιβαίην,
εἰ μή μοι τλαίης γε, θεά, μέγαν ὅρκον ὀμόσσαι
μή τί μοι αὐτῷ πῆμα κακὸν βουλευσέμεν ἄλλο.

(Here is some other thing you devise, O goddess; it is not
conveyance, when you tell me to cross the sea's great open
space on a raft. That is dangerous and hard. Not even
balanced ships rejoicing in a wind from Zeus cross over.
I will not go aboard any raft without your good will,
nor unless, goddess, you can bring yourself to swear me a
    great oath
that this is not some painful trial you are planning against
    me.)

Just seven lines in length, the speech is a masterpiece of tact,
given that the speaker finds himself in a position where he
must question the veracity of the goddess' words. The first
line and the last three are addressed to the goddess. The
three lines in between (174–76) explain his doubts by stress-
ing the danger to a raft crossing the great expanse of ocean.
In short, it is his fear of the ocean, he politely allows Calypso
to believe, *not* his distrust of the goddess, which prompts
him to speak. He can turn a phrase: the personification of the
ships "delighting in a breeze from Zeus" that adorns the center of his speech is light and charming. In being so, it miti-
gates the tone of criticism. The actual request for an oath is
softened in two ways, first by the deferential optatives,

which are not caught in Lattimore's otherwise fine translation,[4] and second by the sentiment immediately introducing the request, namely the affirmation implied in line 177 that he would do nothing against her will. Nothing better expresses the controlled mastery of this speech than the fact that in the Greek text it begins and ends with the same (disarmingly innocuous) word, ἄλλο, meaning "another thing" or "something else." With these few lines alone Homer has sketched a remarkably resourceful human being.

B O O K   S I X

Book six offers a delicate tale of love, the age-old, but never better portrayed, encounter of youthful innocence and middle-aged experience. Nausicaa captivates us. Odysseus, with all his experience of the world, gently takes advantage of her to gain the help he requires, but, in so doing, unavoidably encourages a relationship that cannot be. The tension of this situation adds piquancy to books seven and eight. The book delights not least by its homey atmosphere and sense of family, an atmosphere that stands in deliberate contrast to the grand sweep of the previous book. Odysseus, who at this juncture in the story badly needs the protective nurture of home and family, finds himself in just the situation he needs, except that it is not his home and his family. He must take care not to be drawn in too far.

In Nausicaa Homer presents us a charming portrait of a very marriageable young princess. The book belongs to her and, except for the opening lines of book seven and a short passage in eight, she does not reappear. All the story requires mechanically at this moment is that Odysseus reach the palace and be received kindly. The poet could have ac-

---

[4] Lines 177 and the beginning of 178 might better be translated: "I would not, contrary to your will, board any raft / unless, goddess, you could bring yourself," etc.

complished this in many ways. Nausicaa is far from inevitable. By telling the story as he does, Homer follows up the symbolic rebirth of his hero in book five by giving him in books six to eight the adventures of a young man, principally that of wooing the princess.[5] Presenting Nausicaa first, i.e., before her mother, continues the story pattern established by Homer's presentation of Telemachus, then Odysseus, Peisistratos, then Nestor. The story of the encounter gains somehow in the telling by having as its occasion the most mundane of tasks, doing the family laundry. Instead of work, Nausicaa and her companions make it an outing to the seaside.

Before turning to Nausicaa, the poet injects a strong note of danger; he sounds it in his brief introduction to the Phaeacians (4–12). Lines 4–6 of this passage are most curious, describing the Phaeacians as men

οἳ πρὶν μέν ποτε ναῖον ἐν εὐρυχόρῳ Ὑπερείῃ,
ἀγχοῦ Κυκλώπων, ἀνδρῶν ὑπερηνορεόντων,
οἵ σφεας σινέσκοντο, βίηφι δὲ φέρτεροι ἦσαν.

(who formerly lived in the spacious land, Hypereia,
next to the Cyclopes, who were men too overbearing,
and who had kept harrying them, being greater in strength.)

The Phaeacians, we learn from these lines, used to belong to the fairy-tale world from which Odysseus has narrowly escaped. Like all the denizens of that world, they too pose a threat to Odysseus, perhaps the most dangerous so far. Like Odysseus, they have escaped from the Cyclopes and are their opposites. They are the best seafarers, the most civilized people in the poem, just as the Cyclopes are the most uncivilized and do not know seafaring (9.125–29). They represent the other side of the coin; their civility may be as dan-

---

[5] On the marriage motif in these books, see, for example, Lattimore, "Nausikaa's Suitors."

gerous to Odysseus' homecoming as is the Cyclopes' barbarity. They have potential for harm. The delightful charm of Nausicaa then informs this Phaeacian experience and, for Odysseus, complicates a situation that is already extremely dangerous.[6]

Homer rapidly limns the beauty of his princess by indirect means. We first see her "like the immortal gods in shape and look" (16) asleep in her bedroom. Her surroundings are very beautiful: her chamber is richly decorated (15); her handmaidens have their beauty from the Graces (18); the portals shine (19); and Athena with a delicacy most suited to the occasion comes like a breeze (20). From Athena's words (25–40) we learn Nausicaa's age, just about ready for marriage (27), and that all the best young men woo her (34–35). Note that Athena reminds her of the fine clothes she will need for her wedding (27–28). Homer, in doing this, perfectly suggests her nubile innocence. At her age a wedding means only finery and bliss.

The domesticity of the next scene is compelling. Like the young girl that she is, Nausicaa goes to tell her parents about her dream, particularly her "dear father." She finds them within, her mother weaving at the hearth and her father, like all fathers, on his way to work (53–55), but not too busy for a moment with his young daughter, his favorite. That a special relationship exists between them Homer conveys by the repeated use of "father dear" (51, 56, 57, 67), by having Nausicaa address her words exclusively to him (56), and by his understanding and loving indulgence (66–68).

Ὣς ἔφατ᾽· αἴδετο γὰρ θαλερὸν γάμον ἐξονομῆναι
πατρὶ φίλῳ· ὁ δὲ πάντα νόει καὶ ἀμείβετο μύθῳ·
"Οὔτε τοι ἡμιόνων φθονέω, τέκος, οὔτε τευ ἄλλου."

---

[6] Rose, "The Unfriendly Phaeacians," points out the dangers posed by the Phaeacians.

(So she spoke, but she was ashamed to speak of her joyful
marriage to her dear father, but he understood all and answered:
"I do not begrudge you the mules, child, nor anything
else.")

Homer has given this intimate scene an introduction of stun-
ning beauty. Athena departs for Olympos (42–45),

> ὅθι φασὶ θεῶν ἕδος ἀσφαλὲς αἰεὶ
> ἔμμεναι· οὔτ᾽ ἀνέμοισι τινάσσεται οὔτε ποτ᾽ ὄμβρῳ
> δεύεται οὔτε χιὼν ἐπιπίλναται, ἀλλὰ μάλ᾽ αἴθρη
> πέπταται ἀνέφελος, λευκὴ δ᾽ ἐπιδέδρομεν αἴγλη·

(where the abode of the gods stands firm and unmoving
forever, they say, and is not shaken with winds nor spattered
with rains, nor does snow pile ever there, but the shining bright
air
stretches cloudless away, and the white light glances upon it.)

These lines immediately precede and set the mood for Nausicaa's coming forth from her chamber to meet with her father.

As Nausicaa and her handmaidens set forth on their outing, the poet modifies our perceptions of the princess. She
now has charge of the expedition: she brings the dirty clothes
out and loads them on the wagon (74–75), and she drives the
mules herself (81–82). In short, she here begins to assume a
regal authority so that when the time comes she can play her
role as princess and stand her ground before the rather
frightening castaway who interrupts their game. The poet
completes this transformation with one of his most admired
similes (102–9):

> οἵη δ᾽ Ἄρτεμις εἶσι κατ᾽ οὔρεα ἰοχέαιρα,
> ἢ κατὰ Τηΰγετον περιμήκετον ἢ Ἐρύμανθον,
> τερπομένη κάπροισι καὶ ὠκείης ἐλάφοισι·
> τῇ δέ θ᾽ ἅμα νύμφαι, κοῦραι Διὸς αἰγιόχοιο,
> ἀγρονόμοι παίζουσι· γέγηθε δέ τε φρένα Λητώ·

πασάων δ᾿ ὑπὲρ ἥ γε κάρη ἔχει ἠδὲ μέτωπα,
ῥεῖά τ᾿ ἀριγνώτη πέλεται, καλαὶ δέ τε πᾶσαι·
ὣς ἥ γ᾿ ἀμφιπόλοισι μετέπρεπε παρθένος ἀδμής.

(And as Artemis, who showers arrows, moves on the mountains
either along Taygetos or on high-towering
Erymanthos, delighting in boars and deer in their running,
and along with her the nymphs, daughters of Zeus of the aegis,
range in the wilds and play, and the heart of Leto is gladdened,
for the head and the brows of Artemis are above all the others
and she is easily marked among them, though all are lovely,
so this one shone among her handmaidens, a virgin unwedded.)

This simile reinforces the beauty of the setting, stresses
Nausicaa's regal preeminence, and reminds us of the special
joy that her parents take in her. It does not work as many
Homeric similes do, by making a contrast; rather, it amplifies
on every level the lovely picture we have already received of
this princess. Most especially, the effect achieved here is necessary to prepare for Odysseus' reaction on first seeing Nausicaa (149–85), a reaction that would otherwise risk being
empty hyperbole.

The first 109 lines of this book endow Nausicaa and the
Phaeacians with disarming beauty and with an air of mys-
tery, even danger. The immediate effect in the context is to
create the maximum visual contrast between these lovely
maidens at play in their idyllic land and the begrimed, naked, grizzled wreck of a man who stumbles into their midst.
Their fear at the sight of him (137–39) is understandable; only
Nausicaa with Athena's aid stands her ground. Odysseus
needs help badly. If ever he had occasion to find the right
words, it is now. No speaker, perhaps, has ever found himself at a greater disadvantage. How, standing before this
young thing with only a branch to cover his nakedness and
looking like a ravenous lion, can he hope to gain her confidence? Odysseus earns our admiration with this masterfully

reassuring speech (149–85).[7] With his opening words, he takes care to indicate that he is a civilized man who knows how to make a proper supplication (149), worships the gods on Olympos (150–51), and values highly family life (154–59). He flatters her deftly both by comparing her to the gods, particularly the virgin goddess Artemis, and by using language normally reserved for a goddess to address her. To be specific, he begins the first and third parts of his speech by addressing her as "mistress queen" (ἄνασσα, 149, 175), a word used elsewhere in the Odyssey only by Nestor in a prayer to Athena (3.380). The speech falls into three parts. Gauging shrewdly his young listener, he closes the first and last sections with references to marriage. That man is the luckiest of all who will lead you to his house (158–59). Nothing is better than a happy marriage (182–85).

Though she accedes to his request for help, Nausicaa responds rather primly, even conventionally (187–90).

ξεῖν᾿, ἐπεὶ οὔτε κακῷ οὔτ᾿ ἄφρονι φωτὶ ἔοικας,
Ζεὺς δ᾿ αὐτὸς νέμει ὄλβον Ὀλύμπιος ἀνθρώποισιν,
ἐσθλοῖς ἠδὲ κακοῖσιν, ὅπως ἐθέλῃσιν, ἑκάστῳ·
καί που σοὶ τάδ᾿ ἔδωκε, σὲ δὲ χρὴ τετλάμεν ἔμπης.

(My friend, since you seem not like a thoughtless man, nor a
    mean one,
it is Zeus himself, the Olympian, who gives people good
    fortune,
to each single man, to the good and the bad, just as he wishes;
and since he must have given you yours, you must even endure
    it.)

How different is her reaction a few lines later once Odysseus has bathed and been transformed by Athena. She now notes his similarity to the gods (243). Her confused syntax and abrupt change of subject in lines 244–46 eloquently express her new feelings of attraction and embarrassment.

[7] See also Stanford's treatment of the speech, The "Odyssey" of Homer.

αἲ γὰρ ἐμοὶ τοιόσδε πόσις κεκλημένος εἴη
ἐνθάδε ναιετάων, καί οἱ ἅδοι αὐτόθι μίμνειν.
ἀλλὰ δότ᾽, ἀμφίπολοι, ξείνῳ βρῶσίν τε πόσιν τε.

(Would that such a man might be called my husband, of those
living here I mean, and may it please him to remain here.
But, handmaidens, give this stranger food and drink.)

(My trans.)

The bath and transformation mark Odysseus' successful
completion of the first stage in his acceptance by the Phaeacians.[8]

Athena, acting unseen by Odysseus, has contrived this
meeting on the beach and aided considerably in his initial
acceptance. Although she may help her favorite a little on the
sly, as it were, the hero must in essence get home on his
own. Only then, once he has proved his mettle, does Athena
provide needed aid. The explanation, added at the close of
the book, that the gods respect one another's prerogatives
(329–31) is the storyteller's way of accounting for his virtual
removal from the action of a goddess who otherwise can, in-
asmuch as she is an immortal, do anything she wants. By
leaving the hero more or less on his own, our sense of his
danger is correspondingly greater and an element of suspense is retained.

Nausicaa now takes over from Athena (251)—note that the
phrase used of her, "she had another idea" (ἀλλ᾽ ἐνόησεν),
is otherwise all but restricted to Athena—and gives Odysseus
instructions for the return to town (255–315). As though in
preparation for Ithaca, the situation that Nausicaa describes
sounds at points very like what he will face at home. The
young men are haughty (274) and will see him as a rival (275–
84). He is not to enter the city with her openly, but to come
later so as not to cause idle gossip about a possible relationship between them. She even, in imagining what people

[8] Note the striking parallel with the bath of Telemachus in Pylos (3.464–
68).

might say, puts what are clearly her own hopes into words: "Now he will be her husband" (277). Though she attempts to represent all this as merely a sensible precaution, her syntax betrays her emotion. The temporal clause that begins at line 262 is never attached to a main clause. Rather she breaks off in embarrassment at the imagined shameless behavior of a girl who consorts with men before her marriage (287–88) and begins again abruptly at line 289. Now she changes the emphasis and stresses his *nostos*, return home (290, 311), as though to admit that he is an alien to her world and cannot remain. Is she trying to unsay her previous invitation or does she merely wish to safeguard herself from rejection? However confused Nausicaa may be, Odysseus can scarcely fail to perceive that she looks upon him with real favor as a possible husband. This could pose a serious problem, especially since her father happens to be the local king. It is explicitly the goodwill of her mother and father that he must win in order to get conveyance home (310–15).

While Nausicaa goes into the city, Odysseus sits in the grove of Athena at nightfall and delivers an impassioned prayer (324–27). The tone is not one of confidence. The insistent repetition in line 325 of "hear me" (ἄκουσον before the caesura, the main pause in the line) and "having heard" (ἄκουσας at the end of the line) betrays his desperate state of mind. Odysseus at least knows the danger he faces; the innocent beauty of the princess only heightens the problem. Note that the line he uses to address Athena (324) occurs only one other time in the poem, at line 762 of book four. There Penelope, upon learning that the suitors plan to kill Telemachus, in desperation calls upon Athena for help. Thus book six ends with Odysseus in the grove of Athena. Night has come on (321); the city is close by (294). There is no time to rest; he must press on to meet these people. In this context the last words of his prayer to Athena seem poignant indeed (327):

δός μ᾽ ἐς Φαίηκας φίλον ἐλθεῖν ἠδ᾽ ἐλεεινόν.

(Allow me to come among the Phaeacians as one loved and
    pitied.)   (My trans.)

BOOK SEVEN

Homer uses the seventh book to characterize at length the
Phaeacian court and its king and queen. This court, especially Alkinoos and his wife Arete, not only provides the setting through book twelve, but Odysseus must be accepted by
it in order to get home. He has gained acceptance from the
young princess in the book just preceding by subtly using the
natural inclinations of a young woman who has marriage
much on her mind. The situation now as he comes to meet
the young woman's parents is, to say the least, delicate.
Odysseus handles it with consummate skill, and much of the
enjoyment we derive from this book and the next comes from
watching him skirt dangerous ground. Above all, he must
avoid revealing his identity too soon. He is, after all, a married man. Without ever identifying himself, Odysseus gains
by the end of this book at least conditional acceptance.

The first thirteen lines form a satisfying pendant to book
six. Nausicaa has played her role and must now recede into
the background to re-appear for one brief moment of parting
in book eight. These opening lines provide an excellent example of Homer's swift, rich narrative style.

Ὣς ὁ μὲν ἔνθ᾽ ἠρᾶτο πολύτλας δῖος Ὀδυσσεύς,
κούρην δὲ προτὶ ἄστυ φέρεν μένος ἡμιόνοιϊν.
ἡ δ᾽ ὅτε δὴ οὗ πατρὸς ἀγακλυτὰ δώμαθ᾽ ἵκανε,
στῆσεν ἄρ᾽ ἐν προθύροισι, κασίγνητοι δέ μιν ἀμφὶς
ἵσταντ᾽ ἀθανάτοις ἐναλίγκιοι, οἵ ῥ᾽ ὑπ᾽ ἀπήνης
ἡμιόνους ἔλυον ἐσθῆτά τε ἔσφερον εἴσω.
αὐτὴ δ᾽ ἐς θάλαμον ἑὸν ἤϊε· δαῖε δέ οἱ πῦρ
γρῆϋς Ἀπειραίη, θαλαμηπόλος Εὐρυμέδουσα,

τήν ποτ' 'Απείρηθεν νέες ἤγαγον ἀμφιέλισσαι·
'Αλκινόῳ δ' αὐτὴν γέρας ἔξελον, οὕνεκα πᾶσι
Φαιήκεσσιν ἄνασσε, θεοῦ δ' ὡς δῆμος ἄκουεν·
ἡ τρέφε Ναυσικάαν λευκώλενον ἐν μεγάροισιν.
ἡ οἱ πῦρ ἀνέκαιε καὶ εἴσω δόρπον ἐκόσμει.

(So long-suffering great Odysseus prayed, in that place,
but the strength of the mules carried the young girl on, to the
    city,
and when she had arrived at the glorious house of her father,
she stopped in the forecourt, and there her brothers around her
came and stood, men like immortal gods. They from
the mule wagon unyoked the mules and carried the laundry
inside, and she went into her chamber. There an old woman
of Apeire, Eurymedousa the chamber attendant, lighted
a fire for her. Oarswept ships once carried her over
from Apeire, and they chose her out as a prize for Alkinoos
because he ruled all the Phaeacians and the people listened, as
    to
a god. She had nursed white-armed Nausicaa in the palace.
Now she lit her a fire, and prepared her a supper, indoors.)

In quick succession the young woman reaches the city (line
2), arrives at her father's house (3); her brothers crowd
around her in the forecourt and unload her cart (4–6). We
sense from all this activity that the entire household has been
on the lookout for her. The passage breathes familial love.
Brothers are not always so kind to younger sisters! But Nausicaa is the favorite, beloved by all. Note also how effectively
in the Greek the juxtaposition of Odysseus' name at the end
of line one with the noun "young maiden" (κούρην) at the
beginning of line two underlines their separation. They now
go different ways.

    If the first six lines portray much activity, the next seven
constitute an effective contrast by presenting one picture:
Nausicaa in her own chamber, warmed, loved, and protected. Lines 7 and 13 set the tone; they surround (in the

Greek text) the section with the action of kindling a fire on the hearth. The lines between describe the nurse who looks after her, specially chosen by a loving father. So we leave Nausicaa safe in her chamber. The touch is right; we do not feel that she is neglected or that we are robbed of this delightful creation. Rather, she takes her place in our mind's eye as the backdrop to unfolding events.

Shrouded by the goddess in a mist, Odysseus now comes to the city, where he meets Athena in disguise and is shown to the palace. The parallels between this short journey and Telemachus' journey to Pylos and Sparta are significant and, however lightly, they reinforce the notion that Odysseus here in Phaeacia has the experiences of a young man. In addition, they forward in the audience's mind the growing awareness of the essential similarity between father and son. Like his son, Odysseus is guided by Athena in disguise. She encourages him to be bold (50–52) just as she had put boldness in Telemachus when he addressed Nestor for the first time (3.76). Odysseus marvels at the city (43–45) and the palace (82–83, 133–34) as Telemachus and Peisistratos had marvelled at Menelaos' palace (4.44). Moreover, the same simile is used of Alkinoos' palace and Menelaos' (84 = 4.45). But, since Odysseus in contrast to his son is a man of the world, this palace must be such a one as to justify his admiration; hence the elaborate description of it (84–132). More generally, if Telemachus in book four finds himself in a ticklish situation dealing with Menelaos and Helen, his father here faces the greater challenge of Nausicaa and her parents. These parallels continue in the next book. The opening of book eight at daybreak and summoning of the assembly resemble the situation in Ithaca in book two. Like Telemachus there, Odysseus seeks a ship for conveyance and has difficulty in getting it. As each goes to the assembly, the people admire him and Athena sheds grace on him (8.17–19 are similar to 2.12–13). Each weeps on hearing the story of Odysseus and covers his face (8.84–85, 4.115–16). In addition, each of them hears a version of the story of the wooden horse (8.499–520, 4.266–89). Most importantly, of course, both are soon to realize their true identities.

The Phaeacians live a carefree existence somewhere between the mortal world and that of the gods. They confer upon Odysseus, in providing him a safe and painless journey home, some of their divine happiness, and he confers on them some of his human suffering. His sojourn with them, the poet does not allow us to forget, has its threatening overtones, for like Polyphemos the Phaeacians have a special relationship to Poseidon. Alkinoos is his grandson (61–63). This news can scarcely be heartening to Odysseus and makes his position highly delicate. The threat from Poseidon remains very real.

Homer gives Queen Arete the decisive role by making both Nausicaa and the disguised Athena emphasize that Odysseus must supplicate her first and gain her goodwill if he is to get home. She is thus one of the significant female figures in the poem, figures who first threaten and then help Odysseus on his way. The other two most important are Circe and Calypso. Each superintends one of the major stages in his journey home: Circe sees him off to the underworld and to Calypso, Calypso to Phaeacia, and Arete to Ithaca. Each of these journeys is fraught with symbolism of death and rebirth. It is highly appropriate that females preside over them. This is Arete's role here; she is not grafted on as some memory of Cretan matriarchal rule (though it is possible that she is that too). Nausicaa and Arete together compose the female presence in Phaeacia. The queen takes over from her lovely daughter and poses the major threat to acceptance and to getting home.

Homer devises a dramatic enough first meeting (139ff.).[9] Odysseus appears suddenly from the cloud, makes his sup-

---

[9] On Arete and the many objections posed by scholars to the first encounter at the Phaeacian court, see Fenik, *Studies in the "Odyssey,"* 5–160.

plication to Arete (146–52), and sits in the ashes by the hearth. After a shocked silence Echeneos, the oldest of the advisers, prods the king to take up the stranger from the ashes; thus the poet deliberately forestalls the queen's all-important reaction. Alkinoos has the guest fed (175–77). As if to make up for his initial hesitation, instead of asking the stranger who he is and where he comes from as is standard practice, Alkinoos offers a toast to Zeus, who looks after suppliants (181), and generously proposes that they entertain their guest (190) and send him home all at his ease (191–95). His mood is expansive and he gets carried away somewhat in his enthusiasm (195–98).

μηδέ τι μεσσηγύς γε κακὸν καὶ πῆμα πάθῃσι
πρίν γε τὸν ἧς γαίης ἐπιβήμεναι· ἔνθα δ᾽ ἔπειτα
πείσεται ἄσσα οἱ αἶσα κατὰ Κλῶθές τε βαρεῖαι
γεινομένῳ νήσαντο λίνῳ, ὅτε μιν τέκε μήτηρ.

(And on the way between [he will] suffer no pain nor evil
until he sets foot on his own country; but there in the future
he shall endure all that his destiny and the heavy Spinners
spun for him with the thread at his birth, when his mother bore
    him.)

What a boast! It is as though the Phaeacians have the power to suspend fate for those they convey and, by extension, they themselves are exempt from fate's strong necessity. Alkinoos and the Phaeacians will come to realize, as we shall see in book thirteen, that they too are subject to fate and suffering. The king continues in this mood by boasting that the gods appear to them undisguised. Here he is fishing for Odysseus' identity and, as he does so, Homer makes him sound, as though in warning, a significant negative note. He claims that the Phaeacians in their proximity to the gods are similar to the Cyclopes and savage Giants (206). Their dangerous side always lurks not far below the surface.

Odysseus reacts with studied care. He denies emphatically that he is a god, but rather stresses his great sufferings to elicit sympathy. He hints that he has a good story to tell (213), but forestalls it by pleading that his ravenous belly makes further talk impossible. Let them plan his return tomorrow morning; he would die happily once he has seen home. His pitch for sympathy succeeds and all the others go home for the night (229).

Now at last the queen speaks for the first time; she asks the crucial question that we had expected to hear much earlier: "Who are you of men, and whence? Who gave you this clothing?" (238) The challenge is unmistakable—these last words occur only here. His reply to the suspicious mother had best be a good one. Odysseus recognizes the real interest of the queen and answers only the last question. He recounts at length his adventure with Calypso and his arrival half-dead in Phaeacia (241–97). When at last he gets to Nausicaa at line 290, he places no great emphasis on her, does not in fact mention her name. He concentrates on Calypso as a way of reassuring the queen that he has no interest in her daughter and, when he does refer to Nausicaa, he talks about her the way a parent would a child (292–94). Satisfied as to her main concern, Arete withdraws in silence and does not pursue his identity.

In the next exchange (298–333) Homer broadens the characterization of Alkinoos. He impulsively, without knowing the identity of his guest, offers him the hand of his daughter (313–14). He denies that he is prone to reckless anger (310), yet we know from the pointed question Odysseus has just parried from the queen that it is better by far that he did not show up at the palace with the princess. Let Alkinoos deny it all he wants! He again promises conveyance home in expansive terms, and this time he specifies for tomorrow (318), a promise that is not kept. Alkinoos apparently likes to brag about the prowess of his sailors almost compulsively. More

than half of his speech, lines 317–28, is devoted to it. Homer
thus far has given us a complex and not totally candid character, who is well aware of his superior position of power.[10]
Given the other danger signals present, Odysseus cannot afford to trust him completely.

The final fourteen lines balance the first thirteen by seeing
the rest of the family and Odysseus to bed.

BOOK EIGHT

Book eight brings events to the point where Odysseus can
safely identify himself. It happens slowly, by degrees; the development is subtle. The opening assembly (1–45) provides a
very good example. Alkinoos does not summon it; rather
Athena, in the guise of Alkinoos' herald, takes it upon herself to call the people together (7–14). We are meant to feel
that Alkinoos' hand is being forced a bit as the Phaeacians
come to the assembly to see the stranger. In response Alkinoos does propose conveyance (31), but he prefaces it by a
strong hint that he must know the identity of the stranger
(28–29) and pointedly neglects to specify exactly when the
conveyance is to be provided. Odysseus has made a small
gain, but the situation is still ticklish. To be sure, rowers are
chosen and a ship launched (48–55); but these are routine
acts for a seafaring people that can easily be reversed.

Demodokos now makes his appearance; his blindness has
conferred special status upon him. He and his songs become
the focal point of the book.[11] As a singer, he confers *kleos*,
fame, i.e., a kind of immortality. His singing, therefore, very
appropriately prepares the way for Odysseus' self-identifica-
tion and assumption in books nine to twelve of the singer's

[10] For a different, more positive assessment of Alkinoos, see Austin, *Archery at the Dark of the Moon*, 193–98.

[11] For a useful structural diagram of book eight, see Whitman, *Homer and
the Heroic Tradition*, 289.

role. Demodokos' songs create the atmosphere that brings forth Odysseus' identity.

The first song (73–82) specifically deals with Odysseus at Troy and tells of an otherwise unknown quarrel between Odysseus and Achilles. The language pointedly recalls the opening lines of the *Iliad* and the very bitter, indeed deadly, quarrel between Agamemnon and Achilles. Here the purpose seems to be to set the tone for the harsh encounter between Odysseus and the Phaeacian youths that soon follows (132–233). Moreover, in the narrative the song reminds the Phaeacians of the Trojan War and the heroes who fought in it. Thus they are prepared to hear with peculiar force Odysseus' angry claim (219–20) that only Philoctetes surpassed him in bowmanship at Troy. Though Odysseus' bowmanship is not especially stressed in the *Iliad*,[12] this boast goes far towards identifying him for the Phaeacians. Whoever he is, he is one of the leading Greek fighters at Troy and not a man to be trifled with.

Ever the genial host, Alkinoos moves to smooth over the ruffled tempers (236–55). In deference to his guest and also to soothe him, he imagines him at his home dining with his wife and children (242–43). Dancers and Demodokos are summoned; the latter sings of the adulterous affair between Ares and Aphrodite (266–366). The story breaks the tension by provoking laughter and also by its clear message that forgiveness is necessary. Apologies are proffered and accepted following the song. The conspicuous role of Poseidon as peacemaker at the end of the song (344ff.) must come as a welcome reminder to Odysseus that Poseidon has a side other than the implacable one that he has experienced since he blinded Polyphemos. Surely Odysseus also interprets the song as another warning against trusting a wife, while we the audience perceive it as a story of the unfaithful wife con-

---

[12] In book ten, a book especially marked by trickery, Odysseus is given a bow by Meriones (260). He is not, however, described using it. I thank Professor J. W. Allison for reminding me of this passage.

tained within the saga of the most loyal and faithful of all wives. Odysseus, the clever hero, who has had to learn to use his brains instead of his brawn to defeat his adversaries (Polyphemos, for example), who has used his skill at ship-building to sail away from Calypso, must identify with Hephaistos, who uses his skill at the forge to entrap Ares and Aphrodite. This song, dealing as it does with a story of man and wife, also apparently nurtures a growing realization among the Phaeacians that this hero is married. Note that now also the young Phaeacian Euryalos presumes it in making his apology (410):

σοὶ δὲ θεοὶ ἄλοχον ἰδέειν καὶ πατρίδ᾽ ἱκέσθαι

(May the gods grant it that you see your wife and return home.)
(My trans.)

The quarrel, song, and aftermath clear the air by settling Odysseus' status. Although the Phaeacians still do not know his exact identity, he is clearly one of the leading Greek warriors who fought at Troy and a married man.

By besting the young Phaeacian men in the games, Odysseus has, in the folk motif that underlies these books, won the hand of the princess.[13] Thus the poet now brings her in for a farewell (457–68). He closes this part of the story by recalling in ring composition[14] their first encounter in book six: there Odysseus met Nausicaa first and then was given clothes and a bath, here he is given clothes (441) and a bath (449–56) and then encounters Nausicaa. In his first words to her there he had addressed her as a goddess; here with his last words, he promises to pray to her as a goddess all his days (467–68). There is real poignancy both in the fact that

[13] See, for example, Woodhouse, The Composition of Homer's "Odyssey," 54–65.

[14] Ring composition refers to the frequent occurrence in Homeric narrative of a series of statements, events, etc. arranged in a concentric pattern, the last in the first set being the first in the matching set. It is represented by the schema a b c d d′ c′ b′ a′.

she does not know who he is and that here alone does he address her by name (464).

Demodokos' third song (499–520), like his first, is sung after a feast in the palace, deals with the Trojan War, and evokes tears from Odysseus. Here, now that the Phaeacians, and especially Arete, have sealed the bond of guest-friendship by presenting him gifts (387–445), Odysseus requests the song of the wooden horse, his most famous exploit. By so doing, he explicitly points to his own identity and his readiness to disclose it. His weeping here near the close of book eight (521–22) deliberately balances his weeping at the opening of book five as he sat on the shore longing for home. The simile used to characterize his crying (523–31) movingly underscores the theme of family, particularly the relationship of husband and wife, which is important to the entire poem, but has played an especial role in this book, both in Demodokos' central song and in the growing realization of the Phaeacians that this hero is married.

ὡς δὲ γυνὴ κλαίῃσι φίλον πόσιν ἀμφιπεσοῦσα,
ὅς τε ἑῆς πρόσθεν πόλιος λαῶν τε πέσῃσιν,
ἄστεϊ καὶ τεκέεσσιν ἀμύνων νηλεὲς ἦμαρ·
ἡ μὲν τὸν θνῄσκοντα καὶ ἀσπαίροντα ἰδοῦσα
ἀμφ᾿ αὐτῷ χυμένη λίγα κωκύει· οἱ δέ τ᾿ ὄπισθε
κόπτοντες δούρεσσι μετάφρενον ἠδὲ καὶ ὤμους
εἴρερον εἰσανάγουσι, πόνον τ᾿ ἐχέμεν καὶ ὀϊζύν·
τῆς δ᾿ ἐλεεινοτάτῳ ἄχεϊ φθινύθουσι παρειαί·
ὡς Ὀδυσεὺς ἐλεεινὸν ὑπ᾿ ὀφρύσι δάκρυον εἶβεν.

(As a woman weeps, lying over the body
of her dear husband, who fell fighting for her city and people
as he tried to beat off the pitiless day from city and children;
she sees him dying and gasping for breath, and winding her
    body
about him she cries high and shrill, while the men behind her,
hitting her with spear butts on the back and the shoulders,
force her up and lead her away into slavery, to have

hard work and sorrow, and her cheeks are wracked with pitiful
weeping.
Such were the pitiful tears Odysseus shed from under his
brows.)

The emphasis on the suffering of the wife makes us think of
Penelope, whereas the warlike setting and tragic subject of
the simile particularly suit the sad memories of Troy that
evoked the tears. Finally, it appears meaningful at this point
in the poem that the warrior victorious in the past should
now be compared to his victims. In order to achieve his return home, this warrior has had to learn new ways. This fact
will be made clear in Odysseus' narrative of his adventures.

This book is carefully structured around Demodokos' song
about the love affair of Ares and Aphrodite. In that song, all
is laughter and any damage done is soon undone. The songs
on either side, in contrast, recall Troy and the deadly sufferings of men.[15] Odysseus cries at the recollection. Insofar as
the experience on Phaeacia looks ahead to Ithaca, the harmless, indeed humorous, peccadillos of the immortals remind
us that human transgressions, far from being harmless in the
Odyssey, bring harsh consequences. The eighth book, in
short, not only brings Odysseus to the point where he can
reveal his identity safely, it prepares for the second half of
the epic.

---

[15] The first book of the *Iliad* exploits exactly the same contrast; there the
deadly quarrel between Agamemnon and Achilles at the opening is balanced
by the easily settled domestic squabble at the close between Zeus and Hera.

CHAPTER 3

Books Nine to Twelve

Books nine to twelve are the best-known part of the
Odyssey. In them the hero recounts to the Phaeacians
his adventures. The central adventure, Odysseus' trip
to the underworld, markedly extends his experience. Here he
learns that following death there is only a shadowy, empty
existence for the shades of the departed. This knowledge so-
lidifies his determination to survive. Moreover, it is here in
stating his name and in narrating his wanderings that Odysseus most convincingly establishes his identity. The journey
itself has become by this point in the epic a well-established
metaphor for the acquisition of self-knowledge. Homer
seems to suggest the superior level of Odysseus' knowledge
by depicting him not only as having completed his journey
from Troy to Calypso but as able to recreate it in words. His
very ability to retell his past thus symbolizes his attainment
of self-knowledge. When he has finished his tale at the end
of book twelve, he will have defined his identity for his lis-
teners and will be in a position to do what he in fact does in
the second half of the poem, namely reestablish that identity
to the people in Ithaca.

Odysseus here becomes the singer;[1] the tale is a well-
crafted one with a careful structure. After the sack of the Kikonian city (a doublet of Troy), the adventures fall into two
parallel sets of four. Nonviolent adventures in which no one
dies alternate with violent ones.

1. Lotos eaters
    Oriental motif
    Temptation to forget home
    Odysseus forcibly takes his companions away

[1] For more on this point, see Segal, "*Kleos* and Its Ironies in the *Odyssey.*"

2. Polyphemos

>Monster in a cave
>
>Six men are devoured
>
>Odysseus contemplates using his sword, but realizes he must outwit the Cyclops

3. Aiolos

>Isle of the wind god
>
>Odysseus sleeps
>
>Companions disobey Odysseus
>
>They are blown back, retracing their route

4. Laestrygonians

>Cannibalistic giants: a doublet of the Cyclopes
>
>Odysseus and his ship alone survive; all the others are lost

CIRCE/UNDERWORLD/CIRCE

1. Sirens

>Oriental motif
>
>Temptation to forget home
>
>Odysseus' companions forcibly remove him from danger

2. Scylla (and Charybdis)

>Monster in a cave
>
>Six companions are devoured
>
>Odysseus arms to kill Scylla, but can't even see her

3. Helios

>Isle of the sun god
>
>Odysseus sleeps
>
>Companions disobey Odysseus

4. Charybdis (and Scylla)

>Odysseus alone escapes the storm; all his other companions perish
>
>Odysseus retraces the route to Charybdis: doublet of a sort with Scylla

CALYPSO

The parallelism of the wanderings around the ring composition of the core (Circe/Underworld/Circe) is clear. Each set leads to a female figure to whom Odysseus makes love. Each goddess invites him to stay with her, and each has strong associations with the underworld. Odysseus is progressively stripped in these wanderings of all the trappings that identified him as a leader at Troy, namely his men and ships. The major loss comes in each set after the third adventure.[2] He must, in a sense, lose his previous identity as a warrior and take on a new one. In keeping with this, the poet now depicts prowess in fighting as insufficient for survival; Odysseus must learn in the course of these adventures to resort to his intelligence and cleverness or die.

The parallelism of these journeys nicely suits the overall thrust of the poem, which may best be interpreted as a series of parallel journeys: that of Telemachus to Pylos and Sparta, Odysseus' from Troy to Ithaca via the underworld, and Laertes' from isolated lack of involvement to full involvement with family. Each of these journeys involves growth and/or rejuvenation; each is progressively more metaphorical.

B O O K   N I N E

Book nine begins Odysseus' first-person narrative of his adventures.[3] By making the story of the wanderings a flashback, Homer achieves a number of things. He ends the first half of his poem in a highly entertaining fashion and, by juxtaposing the wanderings with the return to Ithaca, makes them exceptionally vivid. In short, we feel when Odysseus

[2] There are also other organizing principles at work in this narration. Except for the underworld, the adventures are arranged in groups of three, two relatively short followed by a longer one. Thus we have the groupings Kikones, Lotos eaters, and Polyphemos; Aiolos, Laestrygonians, and Circe; Sirens, Scylla (and Charybdis), and Helios. Since the last three adventures in book twelve are told twice, we may also note that there are six accounts of adventures before the underworld and six after. Neither of these alternate schemes, however, accommodates very well the encounter with Charybdis that closes the twelfth book.

[3] On Odysseus as narrator, see M. W. Edwards, *Homer, The Poet of the "Iliad,"* 38–40.

arrives home that he has just come through his adventures.
It requires a conscious effort to remember that he has spent
the last seven years with Calypso.

In telling his own story, Odysseus takes on the role of the
singer. The setting is after dinner (8.473), the most appropriate time for song. Though Odysseus pleads that it is more
pleasant to hear Demodokos than his own mournful tale (1–
15), his account becomes the song, the after-dinner entertain-
ment for the Phaeacians as well as a favorite section of the
poem for hearers ever since. By telling it, Odysseus brings
knowledge of himself, his own *kleos*, to others. *Kleos*, "fame
on the lips of men," equals life for a hero; without *kleos* he is
nothing. Odysseus' act of telling, therefore, has meaning in
terms of this story. By singing about himself, by promoting
his own *kleos*, the *kleos* that he had come dangerously close
to losing on the island of Calypso, he guarantees in a sense
his life and his return.[4] Moreover, by relating his past adventures, he not only tells us who he is, he establishes his identity for himself as well. This is the necessary background for
the return home. He must first know who he is before he can
identify himself to others.

Odysseus experiences much on his wanderings. The first
two adventures in the ninth book, the sack of the Kikonian
city and the Lotos eaters, pose no real threat, though they do
bode ill by presenting his companions as hard to control (44)
and easily tempted. The encounter with the Cyclopes, which
takes up most of the book (105–566), is very different. Odysseus finds himself in a desperate situation where he must
rely on his wits for survival. Though he does win out, he
comes off none too well by his own account. He is to blame
for their predicament (228) and loses six of his own crew. He
then rashly names himself to Polyphemos, laying himself
open to the curse. Although he has overcome Polyphemos
by using his wits, by trickery, the way he identifies himself

---

[4] See above, Chapter 1 note 5, for references to discussions of the meaning
of *kleos*.

to the Cyclops reveals that he has not yet understood the lesson—that he must rely on his *nous*, his wit, his intelligence,
to get home.[5] He boasts to Polyphemos (504–5):

> φάσθαι Ὀδυσσῆα πτολιπόρθιον ἐξαλαῶσαι,
> υἱὸν Λαέρτεω, Ἰθάκῃ ἔνι οἰκί᾿ ἔχοντα.

> (Say that Odysseus *sacker of cities* blinded you,
> son of Laertes, who makes his home in Ithaca.)
> (My trans.)

Here near the beginning of his adventures Odysseus thinks
of himself first and foremost as "city-sacker" (πτολιπόρθιος).
It is as though he were still at Troy. When he at last identifies
himself to the Phaeacians at the opening of this book, he has
completed his wanderings and is about to return home. He
says (19–21):

> εἴμ᾿ Ὀδυσεὺς Λαερτιάδης, ὃς πᾶσι δόλοισιν
> ἀνθρώποισι μέλω, καί μευ κλέος οὐρανὸν ἵκει.
> ναιετάω δ᾿ Ἰθάκην εὐδείελον·

> (I am Odysseus, son of Laertes; all men watch out
> for my trickery, and my fame [*kleos*] reaches heaven.
> I dwell in dusky Ithaca.)   (My trans.)

The change in emphasis is very notable; Odysseus now understands the importance of trickery and its inseparable connection with *kleos*, survival, for him. Book nine provides him
with his first lesson in all this.

    This book takes us to never-never land; the poet modulates
to the world of the fantastic by degrees. The sack of the Kikonian city (39–61) is a doublet of the sack of Troy, a transitional real event, so to speak. Homer uses the storm (67–75)
to suggest the beginnings of helpless disorientation. Note,
however, that it is not the storm, but the simpler, and there-

---

[5] On the connection between the Greek words for mind and return, i.e.,
nous, nostos, and related words, see Frame, *The Myth of Return in Early Greek
Epic*.

fore more mysterious and inexorable, "wave, current, and north wind" (κῦμα ῥόος τε . . . καὶ βορέης, 80–81) that carry Odysseus and his companions off past Kythera into the unknown. The Lotos eaters (84–104) intensify the strangeness and mysteriousness of the world that Odysseus now enters. They are entirely passive and apparently do nothing but eat the lotos and offer it to others. Somnolence pervades the episode. Finally, as Odysseus approaches the land of the Cyclopes, he encounters an uninhabited island, a veritable paradise teeming with goats and fertile meadows (116–51). The night landing there is wholly mysterious and completes the transition. It is pitch black; the ships are enveloped in mist. There is no moon; they can see nothing, not even the line of breakers at the shore. They unexpectedly come aground (142–48). There could be no more eerie entry into the fantastic world of one-eyed giants and cannibals.

The poet takes elaborate care to depict the Cyclopes in some detail as the most uncivilized and barbaric people in the poem. He introduces them to us with a proem of eleven lines (105–15) in which he stresses that they neither practice the arts of cultivation (108–11) nor do they have assemblies or laws in common, but rather live in caves, each a law unto himself (112–15). In short, they do not practice those acts which are the hallmarks of civic life. The description of the untrammeled paradise of goat island immediately follows (116–51). The Cyclopes cannot take advantage of the island's bounty because they have no ships or shipbuilders among them. Neither farmers, nor city-dwellers, nor sailors, they are almost entirely ignorant of human arts.[6] It is no accident, then, that when the poet describes Odysseus blinding Polyphemos, he employs images of seafaring and shipbuilding. The stake used is compared to the mast of a ship (321–24) and the act of blinding to boring a ship's timber (382–86). Odysseus, the man whose skill at raft-building we admired on first

---

[6] Austin, *Archery at the Dark of the Moon*, 143–49, emphasizes their limited intelligence.

seeing him on Calypso's island, here combines skill in using
his hands with cleverness of mind. In the *Odyssey* the one is
a symbol of the other.

Odysseus' celebrated trick in using the name *Outis* (No
One) to deceive Polyphemos (364–412) deserves full appreciation. He gets the Cyclops drunk first, for it is after all a fairly
simpleminded trick that could only deceive a drunken bump-
kin. Odysseus adopts the name in jest; yet it is more true
than he realizes. Try as he might, he can no longer be the
sacker of cities and, in truth, in the underworld and with Calypso he symbolically dies and all but becomes a nobody
(*Outis*). The name possesses another level of meaning. It
came into being as a result of his shrewdness (*mētis* in
Greek), and shrewdness is the very quality he must learn to
rely on for survival.[7] The existence of the negative *outis* ("no
one") in Greek inevitably calls up its reflex, the subordinating
negative *mē tis* ("not anyone"). That Homer means us to
make the connection between *outis* ("no one") and *mētis*
("shrewdness") is guaranteed by his careful wordplay on *mē
tis* ("not anyone") and *Outis* (No One) in lines 405–410, followed by *mētis* ("shrewdness") in 414. Odysseus laughed at:

ὡς ὄνομ᾽ ἐξαπάτησεν ἐμὸν καὶ μῆτις ἀμύμων.

(how my name [i.e., *Outis*] and my utter shrewdness [*mētis*] had
    fooled him.)   (414, my trans.)

He has thus selected a name that implies the quality he must
develop to survive.[8] He is not yet *polymētis* ("full of shrewdness") at the time when he encounters the Cyclops, but he
will become so as a result of his adventures. The name then
is more appropriate than he realizes in both of its senses. The

---

[7] Concerning *mētis* and its range of meanings, see Detienne and Vernant,
Cunning Intelligence in Greek Society.
[8] M. W. Edwards, *Homer, The Poet of the "Iliad,"* 120–21, also points out the
relationship between these words.

joke is not *just* on Polyphemos; the playful irony of the poet is here at its keenest.

This book exploits the themes of the guest/host relationship and eating and drinking. In keeping with his depiction as the most uncivilized character in the poem, not only does Polyphemos not properly entertain his guests with food and drink, he eats them. He also, in his uncouthness, gets drunk, and it is this which brings about his blinding.[9] From the giant's first words (252–55), Odysseus realizes that he and his men are in for trouble. Without so much as a gesture towards offering food and drink, the Cyclops immediately asks them who they are, where they come from, are they perhaps pirates. His words exactly repeat Nestor's questions to Telemachus and the disguised Athena at 3.71–74.[10] There Nestor prefaces his words with a two-line lesson in etiquette (69–70):

Νῦν δὴ κάλλιόν ἐστι μεταλλῆσαι καὶ ἐρέσθαι
ξείνους, οἵ τινές εἰσιν, ἐπεὶ τάρπησαν ἐδωδῆς.

(Now it is a better time to interrogate our guests and ask
them who they are, now they have had the pleasure of eating.)

This careful repetition and omission emphasizes Polyphemos' uncouth behavior. Odysseus tries as hard as he can in his reply (259–71) to remind the Cyclops of the rights that guests and suppliants have in the eyes of the gods. His last two lines form a desperate peroration in which the word for guest/stranger fairly trips over itself in triple repetition—all to no avail (270–71):

Ζεὺς δ᾽ ἐπιτιμήτωρ ἱκετάων τε ξείνων τε,
ξείνιος, ὃς ξείνοισιν ἅμ᾽ αἰδοίοισιν ὀπηδεῖ.

(And Zeus the *guest* god, who stands behind all *strangers* with
    honors
due them, avenges any wrong toward *strangers* and suppliants.)

---

[9] Antinoos, and by implication all the suitors, are the only other characters in the poem who are shown to us drunk. Drunkenness also directly contributes to their downfall; see below, page 127.

[10] These are the only two places where these lines occur in Homer.

The ninth book in summary takes us to the land of make-believe, but it is a threatening, dark land, not one of lollipops and sugarplum fairies. Each movement forward brings a loss, or near loss, and Odysseus and his men sail on "grieved at heart." After the Kikonians, the line "thence we sailed on grieved at heart" introduces each episode up to the journey to the underworld. If the episode before has involved loss of life, the poet adds the line "happy to be alive, but having lost our dear companions."[11] A sense of danger and impending doom overshadows Odysseus and his companions. In such a world one must have one's wits about one at all times to survive.

The tales have a definite rhythm. Book nine contains three adventures, two told briefly and a third recounted at length. Book ten will continue this pattern. Homer means us, I think, to have an awareness of Odysseus as singer, as fashioner of the tale.

B O O K   T E N

While book ten continues the rhythm established by nine, it momentarily at least creates a more positive mood. Odysseus and his men arrive at the island of Aiolos. Everything there is a model of cosy domesticity (5–9):

τοῦ καὶ δώδεκα παῖδες ἐνὶ μεγάροις γεγάασιν,
ἓξ μὲν θυγατέρες, ἓξ δ᾽ υἱέες ἡβώοντες.
ἔνθ᾽ ὅ γε θυγατέρας πόρεν υἱάσιν εἶναι ἀκοίτις.
οἱ δ᾽ αἰεὶ παρὰ πατρὶ φίλῳ καὶ μητέρι κεδνῇ
δαίνυνται· παρὰ δέ σφιν ὀνείατα μυρία κεῖται

(And twelve children were born to him in his palace,
six of them daughters, and six sons in the pride of their youth,
so
he bestowed his daughters on his sons, to be their consorts.

[11] Thus it is that 62 = 105 = 565 = 10.77 = 10.133 and 63 = 566 = 10.134.

And evermore, beside their dear father and gracious mother,
these feast, and good things beyond number are set before
   them.)

It is a very insulated, inbred world, which might well be in-
hospitable to outsiders. To the relief of all, Aiolos entertains
Odysseus for a whole month and graciously sends him on
his way with the winds tied up in a bag (14–27). Things, for
once, could not be going better for Odysseus. The painless
ease of it all, the cosy setting, the following wind dramati-
cally underscore the missed opportunity. To be almost home,
in fact close enough to see details on the shore (30), and then
to be blown back all but destroys Odysseus' morale. He actually contemplates suicide at line 51, an extraordinary
thought for a hero in epic poetry, unparalleled until Vergil.
From this point on, the somber mood of book nine returns,
with the emphasis now not on the threatening circumstances
in the outside world, but rather on the disconsolate attitude
of Odysseus and his men.

The encounter with the Laestrygonians that follows (80–
132) is in some ways a doublet of the Cyclops episode, for
here again cannibalistic giants kill Odysseus' companions.
The similarity makes the difference in Odysseus' behavior
stand out. With Polyphemos he was curious to a fault, wily,
and inventive; at Laestrygonia he is completely resigned and
discouraged. With extreme caution, he alone anchors outside
the harbor (95–96). He takes no direct action and does not
even attempt to help his companions, but flees for his life
(126–32).

The landing in Aiaia, Circe's island, resembles in Odysseus' telling the arrival at goat island. Lack of sound is here
stressed (140) as inability to see was there (9.143–48). Some
god leads the way in each case (141; 9.142). Circe represents,
as did Polyphemos, a major threat to Odysseus. She embodies all the challenges that women can offer to men and then
some, for she has more than human powers. Odysseus

reaches her at his lowest point yet; he has lost all of his other companions. Only he and his own shipmates remain. It is symbolic of their extreme discouragement that after landing they do nothing for two whole days and nights except mope (142–43). Nowhere else in the poem does this happen.

The next scene (144–86) gives Odysseus the strength to go on. He goes to reconnoitre, catches sight of smoke (149), but does not have the heart to search it out (151–55). On his return, however, he kills a stag and brings it back to feed his companions. Instead of a warrior, he here becomes a hunter and, as though to confirm this change, his spear at line 170 becomes a stick to lean on as he carries his load. With this scene then Homer depicts a partial recovery in Odysseus of initiative, in preparation for the role he must play in rescuing his companions from Circe. Despite this, an overwhelming sense of discouragement permeates the entire episode. Odysseus' mention of seeing smoke rising in the middle of the island (196–97), instead of recalling to his companions, as well it might, the smoke of the fires from their own chimneys (see 1.58), causes them to think of the recent horrors of the Laestrygonians and Polyphemos (199–200). Before encountering each they had spied smoke rising up from the landscape (9.167, 10.99). They weep bitterly (201) and continuously (209).

In this mood Odysseus' companions walk docilely into Circe's trap. They apparently have no will to resist. With the aid of Hermes, Odysseus overcomes Circe's magic potion and is invited to the goddess' bed (333–35). Note that he beds her, but, despite the unusually elaborate preparations for eating (348–72), cannot bring himself to break bread with her until she has released his companions (383–87). Had Odysseus taken the act of eating together less seriously and supped *before* freeing his companions, he would never, it is clear, have freed them; for he soon falls so completely under Circe's spell that when his shipmates mention his longed-for goals of return, Ithaca, and fatherland (419–20), Odysseus' only reaction is to repeat mechanically Circe's instructions, "draw your ship up on the beach first of all and store all your possessions and weapons in a cave" (423–24 = 403–4). Finally and only after a year do his companions persuade him to think of home (472). In this way Homer makes it clear that Odysseus barely escaped.

By succumbing to the potion, the outer charms (as it were) of Circe, the companions forfeit any right to her inner charms and therefore have no susceptibility to them. Odysseus, on the other hand, despite overcoming her outward charms, falls victim to the inner, more subtle allure of this enchantress. Odysseus both conquers the goddess and is seduced by her. He remains dependent on her for instructions until after he returns from the underworld. Circe thus presides over his journey to the underworld and has powerful associations with death. Significantly, it is Hermes, guider of souls to the underworld, who leads Odysseus to her and gives him a talisman, the *moly*, to protect him. The *moly*, with its white flower and black root (304), combines opposites, as does Circe. She is born of the sun (138), but leads toward darkness. She both harms and helps. By possessing her sexually, Odysseus in a way brings on his own death, the usual fate of mortals whom goddesses marry (5.118–28). Circe is in a sense a portal to the underworld, and as queen of it must be given a talisman that guarantees the bearer's entrance.

All journeys in the poem become a metaphor for life's journey, the natural goal of which for mortals is death. Thus it is that females oversee these journeys and have dual powers both to help and to destroy. Homer here seems to copy nature, for women, by giving birth, set each of us on the path towards death. Each birth inextricably contains in it the necessity to die; the duality is inevitable. Circe embodies it. Her geographical position, or to be more accurate, her position with regard to the sun reflects her dual role partaking of both light and darkness. Her abode lies between the land of the Laestrygonians, where it is light most of the time (82–86), and the land of the Kimmerians, where it is always dark (11.15–19). In keeping with her mysterious nature, the exact position of her island with regard to the sun remains unfathomable for Odysseus and his men (190–92) until they have been to the underworld, the land of darkness. Upon their return at the opening of book twelve, Circe's island lies where the sun rises (3–4).

After the cosy, homelike atmosphere of the opening lines, a dark gloom settles over the tenth book. Odysseus and his companions are not only disoriented, but basically powerless. They are also dispirited and weep continuously. In fact there is more weeping in this book than any other. The poet injects a mysterious quality into the book by a studied use of vagueness. It is hard to be sure where things are or what they are. The *moly*, for example, not only has mysterious powers, but exactly how Odysseus uses it is left unsaid. Indeed, it is never mentioned again after line 306. Circe's directions to the underworld have the same quality (508–15). She speaks as though Odysseus knows the place well. Of course he does not; he will get there because mysterious powers carry him there, not because he recognizes the street signs, as it were, and knows where to turn. The Elpenor episode (551–60) conveys effectively the same aura of confused uncertainty. Roused suddenly from a drunken sleep and still disoriented, he breaks his neck in a fall from the roof. His loss is the price to move forward. His death probably also reflects a primitive belief in the need of a surrogate to lead the way to Hades, though Homer of course does not use him literally in this way. Odysseus in fact is not even aware, in keeping with the surreal nature of events in this book, that Elpenor is dead. Here his death prepares the audience naturally for the underworld and binds Circe closely to it. Odysseus must return to Circe to give Elpenor burial.

B O O K   E L E V E N

Book eleven presents the journey to the underworld. Its importance is indicated by its placement nearly in the center of the poem. Homer obviously took some pains to achieve this central position for the journey by having Odysseus recount his adventures to the Phaeacians, one of the most elaborate narrative flashbacks in literature. Though book eleven has been much criticized as an inelegant addition, it contributes significantly, all admit, to the poem.[12] Here Odysseus performs the ultimate feat that a hero can accomplish, vanquishing death itself. This journey admirably caps all his journeys by being most explicitly a symbolic death and rebirth. Most importantly, in the larger scope of the epic, it is this journey to the underworld, placed as it is in the structure of the narrative just before his return to Ithaca, which suggests so poignantly that the return home from war for a hero is never easy. He must, in some sense, return from the dead, i.e., die and be reborn.

The book has many memorable passages, particularly the accounts of the individual spirits Odysseus meets. Elpenor, Tiresias, his mother, Agamemnon, Achilles, and Ajax all impress upon us an urgency for life. Odysseus' futile attempt to embrace his mother Antikleia after he has learned that she has died of longing for him (202–8) and Agamemnon's angry sense of loss at not seeing his son before he was murdered (450–53) stand out because of their obvious emotion. But who will fail to respond with warm recognition to Agamemnon's warning not to trust women—present company excepted of course! Virtuous Penelope would never kill her husband (430–46). And so the warning is given from friend to friend with all the niceties observed.

The return to the setting at the Phaeacian court, the inter-

---

[12] Page, The Homeric "Odyssey," 21–51, is the most eloquent of these critics in English.

mezzo (328–84), also has an important function. It reminds us that we are auditors of a narrative and, in preparation for book thirteen, it brings Queen Arete and King Alkinoos again to the fore. Odysseus' tale has impressed. Arete now speaks first (335), something she has not done before. From her words at line 338, "moreover he is my guest" (ξεῖνος δ᾽ αὖτ᾽ ἐμός ἐστιν), we know that Odysseus has finally won over the queen, whose favor was necessary to receive conveyance home. The poet then adds a piquant little scene in which Alkinoos takes over and claims in line 353 that his is the power in this town. The persons who say this in the poem, Telemachus and Alkinoos, though they have a right to it, do not in actuality wield the power in their respective situations. Next Alkinoos calls Odysseus a woman chaser, thief, and liar (364–66) in reaction to Odysseus' transparently polite lie that he would be willing to stay on for a year, if that were Alkinoos' wish (355–61). These are very strong terms, deliberately used with only a thin veil of politeness as a way, apparently, of asserting his superior position. Since Odysseus needs Alkinoos' help to return home, he must acquiesce to this insulting behavior—good training for what he will suffer in his own palace at the hands of the suitors.

In terms of the wanderings, something happens to Odysseus in the underworld to stiffen his determination to stay alive. Before the experience, he contemplates suicide at line 51 of book ten. At that point in his adventures he still had most of his men and ships, those external trappings which secure his status as a hero, a leader of men. At the close of book twelve, despite the fact that he has now lost everything and is alone, he hangs on for dear life to the fig tree above Charybdis. What does he learn in the underworld that gives him this tenacious desire to remain alive?

Circe informs him that he must go there to consult Tiresias, who will tell him about the stages in his return home over the sea (10.539–40). Yet it is Circe who tells him in book twelve about the specific adventures that await him before he reaches the island of Calypso. Some have used this as grounds for supposing that book eleven is added and not quite acclimated to its context. Wrongly, I suggest. Rather, these passages challenge us to look closely at what Tiresias does tell Odysseus and to realize that one goes to the underworld for ultimate knowledge, not to learn relatively trivial things. In short, one does not journey to the underworld to fetch shoelaces. Tiresias tells Odysseus the fundamental things he needs to know, namely that he will get home, that he will kill the suitors, that he must make his peace with Poseidon by making an inland journey,[13] and that death will come to him in peaceful old age with his people prosperous round about him (100–137). Tiresias does, in fact, tell him about his return and about the road and stages of his journey through life. Odysseus learns from the other shades that he encounters about life in the underworld—that it is a shadowy, empty existence and nothing to be desired. This is the knowledge that sustains him in the rest of his trials.

Odysseus gains this perception of death most clearly in his encounters with his mother and with Achilles. He first sees his mother at lines 84–89, but will not let her approach the blood until he has consulted Tiresias. This short scene then motivates him to ask Tiresias why the shade of his mother sits silently and does not know him (142–44). The answer: she and all the ghosts must drink of the blood to know him and to speak (147–49). In Tiresias' case, the blood endows him with the power to speak accurately (96) what a seer speaks, namely the future. To the others it merely confers the

[13] He must put an oar on his shoulder and journey until someone asks him if it is a winnowing fan. He is then to fix the oar in the ground and sacrifice to Poseidon (121–31). In short, he is to bring knowledge of Poseidon to people who have no knowledge of him; he is to extend Poseidon's influence. It is to be an arduous journey, for one has to go a long way inland to find peoples ignorant of the sea in any lands known to Greeks. The oar, the symbol of Poseidon's power, brings the benefits of seafaring, but it also symbolizes the toil of rowing and the sufferings that Odysseus and his men have experienced on the sea. Poor Elpenor had asked just a few lines earlier (77–78) that his oar be set on his tomb. The oar is definitely an ambivalent emblem.

power to speak.[14] Thus, Antikleia has very imperfect knowledge of the current situation in Ithaca. What she says about Telemachus (184–87), namely that he exercises his power as a young squire, is a reasonable assumption based on her knowledge of the situation at the time of her death. At the close of their encounter, when Odysseus tries to embrace his mother's shade, thrice it flees from his hands "like a shadow or a dream" (207). When he blames Persephone, Antikleia explains that this is the way when men die. They have no strength, but (line 222)

$$\psi\upsilon\chi\dot{\eta}\ \delta'\ \dot{\eta}\hat{\upsilon}\tau'\ \ddot{o}\nu\epsilon\iota\rho o\varsigma\ \dot{\alpha}\pi o\pi\tau\alpha\mu\acute{\epsilon}\nu\eta\ \pi\epsilon\pi\acute{o}\tau\eta\tau\alpha\iota.$$

(the soul, dream-like, flitters out and is gone.)

(My trans.)

One can feel in the rapid sounds and images of this line the insubstantiality of death's residue. Achilles, in their encounter (467–540), remains true to his strong characterization in the *Iliad*. To Odysseus' conventional attempt to console him for dying (482–86), Achilles emphatically says he would rather be a slave on earth than king of the dead (489–91).[15] The other shades reinforce this bleak picture by being interested only in what is going on in the upper world. Elpenor requests burial and a tomb so as to be known to those who come hereafter (76).[16] Agamemnon and Achilles want to

---

[14] Much has been made of Homer's inconsistency in this matter of the drinking of the blood. The poet uses it here to strongly mark the lifeless ignorance of the shades. Having done this he has also created a difficulty for himself, for the last of the individual shades he plans to introduce is Ajax, a figure who does not want to speak, at least to Odysseus. The poet carefully avoids the narrative awkwardness of Ajax drinking the blood, an act that indicates an eagerness to communicate, by imperceptibly phasing out the motif. Elpenor, since he is not yet buried, does not drink. Tiresias (95–98), Antikleia (147–53), and the women of the catalog (228–32) do and the act is emphasized in each case with several lines of narrative. After the intermezzo, Agamemnon alone (390) drinks the blood; it is mentioned, as it were, in passing in a subordinate temporal clause. It is then passed over in the case of Achilles so that we do not miss it with Ajax and the rest.

[15] On this scene, see A. T. Edwards, *Achilles in the "Odyssey,"* 43–68.

[16] Some, most notably and vociferously Page, *The Homeric "Odyssey,"* 44–

know about their sons, while Ajax remains angry about the armor of Achilles (544ff.), which was awarded to Odysseus instead of to him. Clearly all that counts is what transpires in the land of the living.

The book has a clear structure. Odysseus recounts in detail his meetings with six spirits and lists more briefly others whom he saw. The intermezzo (328–84) divides them in the middle, three and three. Like the structure of the adventures themselves in books nine to twelve, the poet has arranged these figures in two parallel sets of three (the first three in ascending order of length, the second in descending order) as follows:

1. Elpenor (51–83); 33 lines
    Odysseus speaks first
    Elpenor tells of his own inglorious death and requests
        burial, appealing to Odysseus through his wife and son
2. Tiresias (90–151); 62 lines
    Tiresias speaks first and asks how is it he has come
    Speaks of the situation at Odysseus' home
    Speaks of Odysseus' future
3. Antikleia (152–224); 73 lines
    Antikleia speaks first
    Odysseus attempts in vain to embrace her
    Died because of Odysseus
Catalog of Women (225–327)

Intermezzo (328–84)

46, have complained that there is an inconsistency at the opening of the Elpenor passage (51ff.). Odysseus seems to have known about Elpenor's death and been too busy to bury him on the one hand; on the other, he expresses surprise when he sees him. There is no inconsistency. Lines 52–54 form the explanation that Odysseus gives to the Phaeacians, long after the fact, to account for why Elpenor's body was left unburied in the house of Circe. He then returns to his narrative and gives his direct words on seeing Elpenor's shade in the underworld (57–58). He was surprised at the time, for he had not initially missed Elpenor.

1. Agamemnon (387–466); 80 lines
   Odysseus speaks first
   Agamemnon tells of his own unseemly death and mentions Odysseus' wife and son
2. Achilles (467–540); 74 lines
   Achilles speaks first and asks how it is that he has come
   Asks after the situation at his own home
   Odysseus speaks about the past at Troy
3. Ajax (543–65); 23 lines
   Ajax stands off and so Odysseus speaks
   Odysseus attempts in vain to converse
   Died because of Odysseus
   Catalog of Men (568–627)

The parallelism is obvious. The two catalogs present some problems, the most obvious being that the second contradicts the empty, shadowy image of death that has been the dominant motif in this book. These great figures in the underworld are now shown carrying on a very earthly existence; for example, Minos issues judgments with his golden scepter in hand (568–71). I suspect that all but the lines dealing with Herakles (601–27) are an early rhapsodic interpolation. The lines on Tityos, Tantalos, and Sisyphos, however, were already known to Plato (*Gorgias* 525E). There are problems with the corresponding catalog of women, in which many have detected Hesiodic influence. Lines 240, 249–50, and 286 apparently come from Hesiod's poem *Eioiai* (fragments 30.35, 31.2–3, and 33.12 [West]). Still, some transition is needed to the intermezzo, and the emphasis on women effectively prepares for Queen Arete. Herakles at the close, moreover, provides a useful last paradigm for Odysseus. He is presented as a bowman (607–8) and is helped by Odysseus' particular helpers, Hermes and Athena (626).

Either by their actions or with their words the six major figures remind Odysseus of his mortality and show him that death holds nothing of interest, that the dead are mere insubstantial dreams, and that, even when temporarily endowed with speech, they care only about what is going on, or went on, in the land of the living. The first three figures tell him about his family and his future; the second three represent his past at Troy. At the same time, their interest in their families implicitly or explicitly gives a message to Odysseus about his own. While Odysseus learns that life with all its sufferings is preferable to death, he also here accepts his own mortality. He hears of his death from Tiresias and meets his mother, the one who gave him birth. Birth inevitably implies its opposite, death. In a way, we are perhaps to understand that Odysseus conquers death by accepting its necessity. In any case, he is now prepared to turn down Calypso's offer of immortality, once he realizes that it amounts to nothing more than a living death.

B O O K   T W E L V E

Having taken his hero to the underworld, where he learns from the shades about his own mortality and the nature of death itself, Homer now shows Odysseus resolutely committed to staying alive and returning home. Such is the meaning of the picture with which book twelve ends, namely Odysseus hanging on for dear life to the fig tree overhanging Charybdis (431–41). Trees are a source of life in this poem; one need only mention the double olive under which Odysseus finds shelter at the close of book five and the marriage bed of book twenty-three, fashioned from a living olive tree.

Book twelve brings the adventures to a rapid close. At the same time, Homer neatly avoids any appearance of being perfunctory. By having Circe give Odysseus a private preview of the adventures (37–141) before they happen (166–446), he adds variety to his narrative while conveying the sense of a tale told richly and at leisure. A major purpose of these adventures in book twelve is to dispose of Odysseus' remaining companions. The hero must face the suitors alone;

it won't do to have him sail home with ship and crew. The companions have served their purpose as a supporting cast and now die by knowingly, and therefore foolishly, consuming the cattle of the Sun God. They thus further the theme that men die because of their own foolish actions. In the narrative this reminder comes significantly just as the scene is about to change to Ithaca and provides a natural transition back to the world of the suitors.

At the opening of the book Odysseus and his men return to Circe's island to bury Elpenor. Before the descent to the underworld, this island had been characterized as a mysterious place of indeterminate location with regard to the sun; now that they have (symbolically) died (22), it is described as the place where the sun rises (4). Circe, previously harmful and dangerous, now aids Odysseus and his companions as they set out on their last series of adventures. She tells him the details of the voyage that lies ahead. She thus oversees both the journey to the underworld and the one to Calypso, journeys redolent with symbolic and literal death. Her associations with death remain paramount. Thus it is also that the island of the Sun, her sire (10.138), becomes the most dangerous, and ultimately fatal, test for Odysseus' crew.

Following the extreme discouragement of book ten and his essentially passive experience in book eleven, Odysseus here once again begins to take the initiative. He fails, not through lack of trying, but rather because the gods and his companions thwart his efforts. Circe tells him about the next three major stages in his adventures, namely the Sirens (39–54), the Clashing Rocks and Scylla and Charybdis (59–126), and the Island of the Sun (127–41). In the first case, she gives him precise instructions on how to proceed (47–54). In the second, she says that he himself must make a plan; she will confine herself to telling him the two paths possible (56–58). Nevertheless, her specific discussion of Scylla and Charybdis points clearly (108–10) to the route he should take. In the third instance, she simply states alternative courses of action (to harm or not to harm the cattle of the Sun), but gives no clue as to how to handle the specifics of the situation. Clearly, Odysseus is being encouraged to assert himself more and more.

He does just that. With Circe's help, Odysseus alone has heard the Sirens' song and lived to tell about it. He follows Circe's lead in choosing Scylla and Charybdis, but in facing Scylla he forgets her instructions and arms himself. He tries still to be the warrior of old, but it is utterly in vain. He cannot even see Scylla, much less fend her off. The simile comparing his companions snatched by Scylla to hooked fish (251–55) prepares for a very unusual personal comment from him (258–59):

οἴκτιστον δὴ κεῖνο ἐμοῖς ἴδον ὀφθαλμοῖσι
πάντων ὅσσ᾽ ἐμόγησα πόρους ἁλὸς ἐξερεείνων.

(That was the most pitiful scene these eyes have looked on
in my sufferings as I explored the routes over the water.)

Odysseus rarely in his narrative allows himself a personal aside; thus, he gains immeasurably from these words as a caring leader of men. At the same time the shock of his helplessness also comes through. This artfully prepares the stage for Thrinakia, the island of the Sun. Odysseus tries to avoid the island altogether by warning his companions of the danger (271–76). But he is outvoted and recognizes his helplessness before what the gods have planned (295). Nonetheless, he binds his companions by an oath and does everything in his power to prevent their foolish slaughter of the cattle. The slaughter takes place only when he has been lulled to sleep by the gods (338). When his companions lose their lives in the storm that Zeus sends to punish them, Odysseus steadfastly faces Charybdis alone, riding precariously on the wrecked keel of his ship. Charybdis was the one danger, along with the Clashing Rocks, that Circe in her account advised to avoid at all costs. Even Scylla was preferable. His reach for the fig tree (432), then, not only expresses his commitment to living, but his resourcefulness independent of the goddess. Here and in the storm he improvises for himself and acquires a confidence that he has not possessed since the beginning of the Aiolos episode in book ten. Homer closes the final encounter with Charybdis with the following words (438–41):

ἐελδομένῳ δέ μοι ἦλθον
ὄψ᾽· ἦμος δ᾽ ἐπὶ δόρπον ἀνὴρ ἀγορῆθεν ἀνέστη
κρίνων νείκεα πολλὰ δικαζομένων αἰζηῶν,
τῆμος δὴ τά γε δοῦρα Χαρύβδιος ἐξεφαάνθη.

(To me as I longed for them they came
late. At the time when a man goes from the meeting place to
dinner
having adjudicated the disputes of many vigorous men,
at this time the spars appeared from Charybdis.)   (My trans.)

The idea of returning home after the days' work admirably reinforces our realization that this is the end of Odysseus' narrative. It also particularly suits Odysseus who, now that he has completed his tale for the Phaeacians, is ready to return home. The ambience of the law court looks ahead to his reestablishment of himself as the rightful ruler in Ithaca. One of the primary functions of a king is to adjudicate disputes among his subjects. These lines, therefore, imply the basic change that Odysseus must undergo in the poem. He must move from the fields of Troy, where killing is the norm, to Ithaca, where, once he has rid his house of the suitors, he must rule as king under the law. The passage perfectly prepares for the return to Ithaca in the next book.

CHAPTER 4

Books Thirteen to Sixteen

BOOKS THIRTEEN TO SIXTEEN bring Odysseus and Telemachus back to Ithaca from their roughly parallel journeys; Odysseus returns in book thirteen and Telemachus in book fifteen. After their reunion in the sixteenth book, they begin to plot the destruction of the suitors. This section of the poem thus further develops the theme of father and son and brings into prominence the themes of disguise and recognition. Except for the opening lines of books thirteen and fifteen, which are set respectively in Phaeacia and at Sparta, these four books take place in the countryside of Ithaca, primarily at the steading of Eumaios.

Not much happens in these books, it must be pointed out, to advance the story line, and what does occur could be told in short compass. Besides the fact that it is in the manner of a good storyteller to develop his tale in leisurely fashion so as to let his audience savor the details, Homer appears here to slow down the action on purpose, as a way of impressing on his audience the care that Odysseus must take to regain his rightful place in Ithaca. These books present the first stage, in which Odysseus ingratiates himself with one loyal servant, the swineherd Eumaios, and finds in his son an ally.

Athena, the protectress of Odysseus and his family, returns to the fore in book thirteen, and in a highly charged encounter Odysseus reveals himself as a match for the goddess in wits. In the next book he finds that his planned strategy must be altered because his allies in Ithaca believe him dead. By the end of the book he adroitly begins to gain Eumaios' confidence. The focus then switches to Telemachus, who reveals himself in book fifteen as able to make difficult decisions, but also liable at the prospect of action to give way to excitement. In book sixteen, however, Telemachus handles himself with remarkable control when face-to-face with his father and, in fact, refuses to acknowledge him until he receives adequate proof. In some sense, he shows himself his father's equal. The poet thus stresses in these books the shrewdness of both Odysseus and Telemachus.

Telemachus, who had left Ithaca under the guidance of Athena/Mentor, comes home as captain of his ship, bringing a suppliant whom he has taken in. He has become a leader of men, a lesser Odysseus. In contrast, Odysseus, who had left Ithaca at the head of a contingent of ships, returns alone, a passenger on someone else's vessel. He has passed through fire, we know, and has attained a heroism open only to the greatest heroes. The reunion between father and son, whom Homer again and again has portrayed as very much alike, constitutes one of the great moments leading to the denouement. The poet carefully builds to it, giving it to us only in the last book of this tetrad.

BOOK THIRTEEN

The opening scenes of book thirteen (1–187) bring Odysseus at last to Ithaca. Ideas of home and family introduce the journey. The poet further emphasizes the moment with a simile (31–35):

> ὡς δ' ὅτ' ἀνὴρ δόρποιο λιλαίεται, ᾧ τε πανῆμαρ
> νειὸν ἀν' ἕλκητον βόε οἴνοπε πηκτὸν ἄροτρον·
> ἀσπασίως δ' ἄρα τῷ κατέδυ φάος ἠελίοιο
> δόρπον ἐποίχεσθαι, βλάβεται δέ τε γούνατ' ἰόντι·
> ὡς 'Οδυσῆ' ἀσπαστὸν ἔδυ φάος ἠελίοιο.

(And as a man makes for his dinner, when all day
long his wine-colored oxen have dragged the compact plow for
   him
across the field, and the sun's setting is welcome for bringing
the time to go to his dinner, and as he goes his knees fail him;
thus welcome to Odysseus now was the sun going under.)

This simile accomplishes several things. Drawn as it is from country life, it begins the transition to the predominant setting for this part of the poem, the countryside of Ithaca, particularly the abode of Eumaios, the swineherd. It especially enhances our appreciation of Odysseus' longing to be homeward bound, his great weariness, and the heartfelt relief he will derive from finally getting home. For the moment the dangers posed in Ithaca by the suitors recede into the background before these positive images of home. Odysseus now speaks for the last time to Alkinoos (38–46) and to Arete (59–62). Appropriately, his last words at the Phaeacian court, as his first (7.146–52), are addressed to the queen, and even more appropriately, his last thoughts are of family. He wishes that each may prosper in spouse and children. With these very personal sentiments he departs for home.

In contrast to Odysseus' previous journeys, this voyage is painless. He passes it in a deep sleep, a sleep specifically likened to death (80). The Phaeacians deposit him still asleep on the shore near an olive tree and a cave of the nymphs (102–5, 119–22). Trees are always life-giving in this poem; caves have a dual aspect. Persons who inhabit them have the power to hurt (Polyphemos) and to help (Calypso). Caves naturally imply the dual symbolism of womb and tomb. This cave, a cave of the nymphs and a repository of honey, has all the positive images of feminine nurturing. Here, as Odysseus arrives at his homeland, are clustered numerous images of rebirth—journey over water, daybreak, awakening, the cave, and the olive tree. This journey is nicely associated with the symbolism of death and rebirth, for his fellow Ithacans believe him dead and to many of them he will seem literally to have come back from the dead.[1]

The pain of this last journey is transferred to the Phaeacian crew, who are turned to stone by Poseidon as they sail into

---

[1] And, on the level of the narrative structure, Odysseus *has* returned from the dead, with the journey to the underworld in book eleven placed so close in the telling to the return to Ithaca in book thirteen.

their home harbor. Before punishing them Poseidon consults Zeus (125–60). The parallel with the meeting between Zeus and Athena in book one is deliberate. Poseidon now, not Athena, is frustrated by the situation regarding Odysseus, and he is allowed to vent his anger on the Phaeacians as his final act in the poem. Note that he is mentioned only three times more, each time in passing (23.234, 277; 24.109). Now that Odysseus is no longer in Poseidon's domain, Athena is, as the poet has made a point of indicating, at last free to act; an important stage has been reached here at the beginning of the second half of the poem.

The opening scenes do much to suggest a sharp break and a new beginning. On a stylistic level, the poet marks the beginning of the second half by using phrases in lines 5–6 and 90 that recall the proem of book one, phrases that stress the many sufferings and wanderings of Odysseus. In addition, Poseidon's punishment of the Phaeacians and putting an end to their escort service distances it all. It is a storyteller's device to explain why Odysseus was the last and why things like this no longer happen. The sense of bringing the journeys, and the many sufferings associated with them, to a close is powerful here. The story now continues at a more leisurely pace. We have not up to this point in the poem had the opportunity to observe Odysseus and Athena interact much. Since their relationship is crucial to the rest of the poem, the poet now seizes the opportunity to portray it in detail.[2]

From the outset Athena tests Odysseus' mettle. She appears to him in the disguise of a young herdsman (222) and does not reveal her identity for many lines (300). Her veiling of the countryside in mist (189) causes Odysseus to feel be-

---

[2] The placement at this point creates a structural parallel between father and son. One can only admire the control that places this encounter at the beginning of the second half so that it balances the meeting between Telemachus and Athena in book one. My own analysis of this meeting between Odysseus and Athena owes much to Clay, *The Wrath of Athena*, 186–212.

trayed by the Phaeacians. Having put him in this distrustful
state of mind, the goddess then tries, by appealing to his ego,
to trick him into proclaiming his identity prematurely. For, to
his direct question, "what land is this" (233), she makes a
reply calculated to tease (237–49), leading from the statement
that everybody knows to a description that particularly fits
rugged Ithaca—one can picture Odysseus' growing excitement as this description proceeds—to a final boast that the
name of Ithaca has gone even to Troy! Clearly Athena is trying to tempt him via his pride into declaring that he is King
Odysseus, the very man who has carried Ithaca's fame to
Troy. Odysseus does not fall into her trap. Instead, he dis-
sembles; his tale of deception (256–86) is the first of a number
in the second half of the poem. In each he claims to be from
Crete, and each is carefully tailored for the particular occasion. Here Odysseus issues a pointed warning (259–62) designed to discourage the young man from any thought of
stealing the treasure, which he has not yet had time to hide
in a safe place.

> φεύγω, ἐπεὶ φίλον υἷα κατέκτανον Ἰδομενῆος,
> Ὀρσίλοχον πόδας ὠκύν, ὃς ἐν Κρήτῃ εὐρείῃ
> ἀνέρας ἀλφηστὰς νίκα ταχέεσσι πόδεσσιν,
> οὕνεκά με στερέσαι τῆς ληΐδος ἤθελε πάσης

(I have fled, an exile, because I killed the son of Idomeneus,
Orsilochos, a man swift of foot, who in wide Crete surpassed
all other mortal men for speed of his feet. I killed him
because he tried to deprive me of all my share of the plunder.)

Tangible goods are the outward signs of Odysseus' standing
in the community. As such they are very important to him.
His readiness to kill to preserve them here foreshadows the
attitude he will have towards the suitors and their wanton
consumption of his property.

Threatening gods, even gods in disguise, is tricky business. Athena's reaction is bemused admiration (291–95). She

praises his cleverness, but chides him for not recognizing her, the one who has been continually by his side helping him. Odysseus' reply (312–28) sets the precise tone that Homer wishes to establish for his hero. Instead of showing subservience now that he knows who she is, Odysseus replies in kind. He points out that she is hard to recognize even for a very experienced fellow since she can take on any form; i.e., her criticism is not justified. He then goes on the offensive by challenging her claim of continually helping him (314–18):

τοῦτο δ᾽ ἐγὼν εὖ οἶδ᾽, ὅτι μοι πάρος ἠπίη ἦσθα. . . .
αὐτὰρ ἐπεὶ Πριάμοιο πόλιν διεπέρσαμεν αἰπήν, . . .
οὐ σέ γ᾽ ἔπειτα ἴδον, κούρη Διός. . . .

(But this I know well: there was a time when you were kind to
    me. . . .
But after we had sacked the sheer citadel of Priam, . . .
I never saw you, daughter of Zeus. . . .)

And in line 323 he contradicts her by pointing out that in any case he did recognize her (αὐτή, "you yourself") in Phaeacia. Placed on the defensive, she makes the lame-sounding excuse that she did not want a fight with Poseidon (341–43)[3] and removes the mist that shrouds the true appearance of Ithaca (344–51).

Homer depicts Odysseus in this encounter as Athena's equal. His stature is enhanced, not diminished, in the presence of the goddess. We understand why Athena admires him and why he is her special favorite. He is a strong hero, not some cipher who gains his victory simply by being the tool of the gods. Odysseus and Athena plan the destruction of the suitors together as close partners. The use of the duals

---

[3] The poet himself has supplied this explanation in 6.329–31 as a way of motivating his decision not to have Athena aid Odysseus openly until he reaches Ithaca. Thus, although the excuse is true in terms of the narrative, it will hardly appear as more than an arbitrary choice to Odysseus.

in lines 372 and 373 seems intended to reinforce this.[4] Even
after the partnership has been established, Homer takes
pains to stress Odysseus' independent spirit. Note that the
hero cannot resist a pointedly critical remark when Athena
mentions that Telemachus has gone to Sparta for news of
him (417–19):

> τίπτε τ' ἄρ' οὔ οἱ εἶπες, ἐνὶ φρεσὶ πάντα ἰδυῖα;
> ἦ ἵνα που καὶ κεῖνος ἀλώμενος ἄλγεα πάσχῃ
> πόντον ἐπ' ἀτρύγετον, βίοτον δέ οἱ ἄλλοι ἔδουσι.

(Why then did you not tell him, since in your mind you know all
   things?
Was it so that he *too* wandering over the barren
sea should suffer pains, while others ate up his substance?)

Understanding his deep concern for his son, Athena reassures him of Telemachus' safety and firmly corrects him. She
sent him on that journey to gain *kleos* (422), the primary attri-
bute of a hero. He cannot quarrel with this purpose.

Athena now disguises Odysseus as an old beggar and
sends him to Eumaios, while she herself goes off to Sparta to
fetch Telemachus (440). The disguise, the guile behind it,
suits Odysseus;[5] it is the natural expression of what he has
learned on his journeys, i.e., to use deception, to survive by
his wits, his cleverness. It is also the sort of thing he has done
at Troy in the past (4.244–50), and his patron goddess is the
master of it. In fact, her disguise at the beginning of this book
has offered an excellent example of its efficacy. In the poem,
only she and Odysseus adopt disguises. Here the disguise is
in fact a complete transformation of outward appearance.
Odysseus is made to look like an old man, but he retains the
strength of a hero. He cannot, however, undo the change in

---

[4] Duals are special endings in Greek that are normally restricted to things
that are natural pairs, such as eyes. The use of duals here suggests the bond
between Odysseus and Athena.

[5] See on the general theme of disguise, Murnaghan, *Disguise and Recognition in the "Odyssey."*

his physical appearance without Athena's help. Her transformations of him back to youthful middle-age mark important points in the narrative in the second half of the poem and are among the ways the poet continues the motif of rebirth and rejuvenation. Finally, the disguise provides a most satisfying means to allow Odysseus to move among his own people undetected. We, the audience, take great pleasure in our and the hero's superior knowledge.

BOOK FOURTEEN

We now follow Odysseus to Eumaios' steading, where we find the swineherd making a pair of sandals (14.23–24). The detail is telling. Like his master this man works skillfully with his hands. He has cared well for his master's pigs and resents being forced to send them to the palace for the suitors (27). From his first words (37–47) Odysseus can have no doubt of his loyalty. Eumaios mourns him almost unnaturally and speaks of him almost constantly (40–44, 61–71, 90–104, 133–47). He is clearly proud to serve such a lord; in fact, he regards Odysseus with greater affection than he does his long-lost parents (140–44). His feelings for him are so great that he can scarcely bear to utter his name. Only the direct query from Odysseus in lines 115–18 draws it out at last at line 144.

Here with Eumaios, Odysseus encounters for the first time one of the greatest obstacles with which he must contend—namely, the despair of those loyal to him and their disbelief in any prediction that he will return. They have been disappointed too often in the past by false rumors and do not want to suffer further disappointment. They therefore do not want to hear, and adamantly refuse to believe, any reports of Odysseus' return. From the start, Eumaios speaks of Odysseus as one gone for good (see lines 40, 61, 68, 90, 133–37). He even warns the beggar directly not to abuse his mistress by telling lying tales about his master's return (122–30), even before he has said who his master is! It is important to realize in what a difficult position this places Odysseus. His basic strategy is going to be, we see from his actions, to gain the confidence and the support of those loyal to him without revealing his identity. One of his strongest weapons to rally support against the suitors, however, was to be the careful deployment of the prediction that Odysseus is nearby, indeed expected at any moment. He clearly planned to lend credence to his report by providing corroborative details as the situation demanded. Now he finds that people are unwilling to listen to such talk.

Eumaios, for example, denies the report politely enough and changes the subject the first time Odysseus tries it (166–90). When he works it in again near the end of his life story at lines 321 and following, the swineherd politely, but unmistakably, calls him a liar (363–65) and makes it clear that he has no patience for such stories any longer (378–87). Odysseus wisely changes his tack in his last tale in the book (462–506). He uses the need for a mantle as an excuse to weave a story set at Troy. In it, he, Odysseus, and Menelaos lead a night ambush, during which Odysseus cleverly saves him from the freezing cold. The story tells Eumaios much about his guest and proves that he knows Odysseus and knows him well indeed. That is the raison d' être of it, not merely to secure the loan of a mantle for the night. He could simply have asked for one and it clearly would have been provided. Eumaios is a model host. To this final tale, the swineherd responds very warmly (508ff.) with a promise made in Telemachus' name of new clothing. This promise marks a wholly new, deeper, level of acceptance.[6]

The central section of this book (191–359) is devoted to the deceitful tale that Odysseus tells about himself in response to Eumaios' request to know who he is. He will have occasion to tell several such tales in the coming books (see especially

[6] The words Eumaios uses at lines 510–11 to make the promise nearly repeat Nausicaa's initial words (6.192–93) to Odysseus after his masterful speech to her. The echo increases the warmth of the response.

17.419–44 [to the suitors], 19.165–202 [to Penelope], and 24.302–14 [to Laertes]). They reveal something of his devious character to be sure.[7] Note the gentle irony of the identity Odysseus adopts—throughout his tales he claims to be Cretan, that is, a member of a people famed for being the best liars in the world. In general his tales have not received the appreciation they deserve. They become his primary tool in eliciting the response he wants, and he carefully tailors each story to suit the hearer in question. Here in book fourteen, Odysseus wishes to ingratiate himself with Eumaios, so he devises an elaborate and entertaining tale of adventure. It is a story that takes him from Crete to Troy to Egypt to Phoenicia to Thesprotia and finally to Ithaca. Wars, shipwreck, and being shanghaied by villains enliven it. Most of all, since he has the advantage of knowing Eumaios' life story, he carefully makes his story bear a close resemblance to Eumaios' actual experiences on two major points. He claims to have been, like Eumaios (15.403–14), the son of a wealthy nobleman (200) who has fallen on bad times. In addition to hard luck in battle, the chief reason for his current misfortune is the treachery of a Phoenician man who kidnapped him on a sea voyage intending to sell him into slavery (288–98). It was of course Phoenician traders who treacherously kidnapped Eumaios and brought him to Ithaca (15.450–84). By this means Odysseus guarantees a sympathetic hearing. How can Eumaios see him as anything other than a soul mate?

The tale is very elaborate, perhaps the most elaborate and entertaining of all his stories. The two old men, after all, are passing time (see 193–95 and 15.390–94). Only the double deception and kidnapping, first by the Phoenicians and then by the Thesprotians, seem a little contrived, a way to work in Odysseus and still account for the beggar getting to Ithaca. The poet, I think, has done this deliberately in order to make

7 Murnaghan, *Disguise and Recognition in the "Odyssey,"* 166–68, exploits the notion that they recast Odysseus' actual experiences.

the audience feel that Eumaios' disbelief is justified and, as a device of characterization, to portray Odysseus as laboring some in this extended tale. He has not completely rehearsed it and worked it all out, but rather is improvising. The poet's deployment of these predictions of Odysseus' return also becomes an important narrative device in books fourteen to twenty-one to build up the hero's long-awaited self-revelation to his enemies.

Odysseus finds in Eumaios a safe haven, a good servant who loves him and his family. The swineherd greets him warmly and takes him in, beggar though he is, and offers him all hospitality. The role reversal of servant entertaining master creates a friendly, sometimes humorous, atmosphere. Odysseus' experience with Eumaios both reassures him that he still has some loyal servants and justifies his harsh treatment of those disloyal to him. The entire scene, in fact, underscores the disloyalty of the suitors and their servants and thus provides the necessary prelude to the goings on at the palace.

BOOK FIFTEEN

The fifteenth book brings Telemachus back to Ithaca in preparation for the recognition scene with his father. The book begins abruptly and emphatically. Athena goes to Sparta to remind Telemachus of his return and specifically instructs him, once he reaches Ithaca, not to go to the city, but to go first of all to the swineherd (36–40). No explanation for this strange order is offered. The importance of the moment, however, is stressed by the fact that Telemachus, though lying in bed, is awake (7), and Athena appears to him apparently in her own likeness. No disguise is mentioned. She scarcely grants this privilege even to his father. Telemachus is so stirred by Athena's words that he wants to start at once (46–47), and Peisistratos must remind him that Menelaos ought to have the opportunity for a proper goodbye (49–55).

The point is not to imply that Telemachus has suddenly forgotten all he has learned, but rather to stress vividly the overwhelming effect that this visit from Athena has had on him. The word used for Telemachus' return at the beginning of line 3 is *nostos*. Elsewhere in the poem it is used of the return home from Troy. The usage here definitely elevates Telemachus' return to the level of his father's. Note, in keeping with this, that his final words to Helen as he departs, wishing that her prediction of his father's return might be true (180–81), repeat Odysseus' final words to Nausicaa (180 = 8.465; 181 = 8.467). In general, their encounters with these women have other similarities. The younger man, for example, has met an older woman in a context of marriage; the older man encounters a younger woman in a context that has all the aspects of courtship. And each has, in a very different way, found himself in a family situation that has required the utmost tact.

This book picks up and reemphasizes Telemachus' growth. He is now sure enough of himself that he can appreciate the necessity of avoiding unwanted hospitality. By rights he should return with Peisistratos to Nestor. But he needs to get home and he knows that a visit to the garrulous old gentleman will only delay him. After all, Telemachus has just had proof of this, for, despite Menelaos' protestation of understanding, Telemachus did have some difficulty in getting away from Sparta (64–153). He therefore persuades a reluctant Peisistratos to leave him at his ship (195–214). But it is with Theoklymenos that Homer marks most clearly Telemachus' status as a mature leader.[8] Theoklymenos comes to him as he is about to embark (222–25). To underline his importance the poet gives him an unusually long pedigree (225–55): he is a prophet from a long line of prophets whose ancestral home is Nestor's Pylos (226). As a prophet, he is a

---

[8] On Theoklymenos and the vast literature surrounding him, see Fenik, *Studies in the "Odyssey,"* 233–44.

holy man who would be wearing some visible symbol of his status, perhaps fillets. He is also a fugitive who has killed a man. Murderers in the ancient world were considered polluted and were restricted on penalty of death from certain holy places on the grounds that they would contaminate them. This man, then, asks Telemachus to take him as a suppliant on board ship (277–78). He reeks of numinous power, both positive and negative; he is certainly a dangerous companion to have on a sea voyage. That Telemachus has the confidence to take under his protection as a suppliant such a figure sets him apart as a full-fledged leader of men. Moreover, we must not miss that Telemachus here assumes Nestor's role, for Theoklymenos most certainly has come to his ancestral home in the first place to seek refuge with King Nestor.

As Telemachus sails, the poet shifts the scene back to the steading of the swineherd and to Odysseus (301–492). In the encounter that follows, he shows that Odysseus has gained the confidence of the swineherd. Odysseus now proposes that he go to town to beg, to bring a message to Penelope, and to mingle with the suitors. Eumaios reacts to this very strongly by pointing out that he will bring down destruction on himself, if he tries to go among the overbearing suitors (326–29). He no longer, it should be noticed, tries to dissuade the beggar from talking to Penelope, as he had done when they first met (14.122–32). His concern is now primarily for the beggar, whom, by his invitation to stay with him, he implicitly takes under his protection. Odysseus welcomes the opening and agrees to stay in the most friendly terms possible (341–42):

αἴθ᾽ οὕτως, Εὔμαιε, φίλος Διὶ πατρὶ γένοιο
ὡς ἐμοί, ὅττι μ᾽ ἔπαυσας ἄλης καὶ ὀϊζύος αἰνῆς.

(Would, Eumaios, that you were so dear to father Zeus as you
are
to me, since you stopped my wandering and terrible suffering.)
(My trans.)

With these words Odysseus takes the swineherd as his protector.

In keeping with his strategy to talk of Odysseus as much as possible, he now asks Eumaios about Odysseus' mother and father (347–48). That he dares to ask personal questions about the family illustrates his new position as a member of Eumaios', i.e., Odysseus', larger household. Eumaios responds by telling of his favored status with Odysseus' mother. Following this lead Odysseus next inquires after Eumaios' own parents and his life story. He of course knows the answers to all that he asks; by these questions he is attempting to instill in the swineherd a feeling of closeness to him. Eumaios' words at lines 398–401 clearly reveal his success.

νῶϊ δ᾽ ἐνὶ κλισίῃ πίνοντέ τε δαινυμένω τε
κήδεσιν ἀλλήλων τερπώμεθα λευγαλέοισι,
μνωομένω· μετὰ γάρ τε καὶ ἄλγεσι τέρπεται ἀνήρ,
ὅς τις δὴ μάλα πολλὰ πάθῃ καὶ πόλλ᾽ ἐπαληθῇ·

(But we two, sitting here in the shelter, eating and drinking,
shall entertain each other remembering and retelling
our sad sorrows. For afterwards a man who has suffered
much and wandered much has pleasure out of his sorrows.)

Eumaios now regards the beggar with empathy as someone to whom he can tell his life story (402–84).

The book closes, quite unusually, at dawn (495), with Telemachus' arrival on Ithaca.[9] Telemachus sends his companions on to the city and says only that he is going to visit his fields and herdsmen (504). His care in not specifying exactly where he will be suggests that he knows something is up,

[9] Note the parallel with his father's return at daybreak in book thirteen. The twenty-third book is the only other of this poem to close with the dawn. There dawn marks the end of the unusually long night that Athena has given Penelope and Odysseus to enjoy. The coming of dawn marks the necessity to face the issues that press in on them, primarily the expected retaliation from the relatives of the suitors. Another reason that book twenty-three ends with the coming of daylight is that the poet seeks a contrast with the final book, which is to begin with a scene in the underworld.

that he suspects Athena has some special purpose in sending
him to Eumaios. Moreover, his excitement is portrayed by
the fact that he neglects to provide for his guest, Theoklymenos, who must ask where he should go (509). His first impulse is to send him to Eurymachos' house, on the ground
that he is the best of the suitors. To do this would be, we
realize, to renounce his newly established position as leader
of men; the fact that he even contemplates it reveals how
threatened he feels by the situation in Ithaca. Before he can
act—in fact, before he finishes speaking—a hawk appears on
his right, a portent that Theoklymenos interprets as meaning
that Telemachus' house is the most royal in Ithaca (533–34).
Buoyed by the omen, Telemachus now asks one of his followers to take him in, thus asserting his rightful role as continued protector of the seer. This portent on landing matches
the appearance of the eagle as he was about to depart on his
return journey (160–65). Portents thus frame his return, mag-
nifying the stature of Telemachus as he is about to encounter
his father.

BOOK SIXTEEN

Book sixteen reunites Telemachus and Odysseus. It also
looks ahead to the next part of the story by giving us a vivid
scene of the suitors at the palace (321–451). The first 155 lines
set the stage for the recognition and reunion between father
and son. Telemachus arrives at the swineherd's steading,
and Eumaios is sent off to bring the news of his safe return
to Penelope, thus leaving Telemachus and Odysseus alone.
The poet also uses these lines to prepare us for the reunion
by giving us a preview. Eumaios greets Telemachus very
warmly (17–21).

> ὡς δὲ πατὴρ ὃν παῖδα φίλα φρονέων ἀγαπάζῃ
> ἐλθόντ᾽ ἐξ ἀπίης γαίης δεκάτῳ ἐνιαυτῷ,
> μοῦνον τηλύγετον, τῷ ἔπ᾽ ἄλγεα πολλὰ μογήσῃ,
> ὣς τότε Τηλέμαχον θεοειδέα δῖος ὑφορβὸς
> πάντα κύσεν περιφύς.

(And as a father, with heart full of love, welcomes his only
and grown son, for whose sake he has undergone many
   hardships
when he comes back in the tenth year from a distant country,
so now the noble swineherd, clinging fast to godlike
Telemachus, kissed him.)

The simile requires us to think of Odysseus and to expect a
similarly heartfelt reunion. But Homer has a surprise for us.
Telemachus next inquires after the stranger (57). On hearing
that he is his suppliant (67), Telemachus responds in
astounding fashion. This after all is the same man who in the
book just preceding had the confidence to accept the fugitive
Theoklymenos as a suppliant. It is as though the apron
strings reassert themselves and Telemachus loses his confidence as soon as he sets foot on Ithaca. In any case, he refuses to take in the suppliant on the grounds that he cannot
protect him given the situation in his own house (69–72, 85–
89). No matter how prudent, Telemachus as head of the
house in his father's absence should not refuse a suppliant.
Odysseus can scarcely believe his ears. Can this be the son
he has longed to see for nearly twenty years?! He challenges
and rebukes Telemachus by wishing that "a son of blameless
Odysseus were present" (100). He, in fact, is so incensed that
at lines 105–7 he says, with only the thinnest veil of disguise:

εἰ δ᾽ αὖ με πληθυῖ δαμασαίατο μοῦνον ἐόντα,
βουλοίμην κ᾽ ἐν ἐμοῖσι κατακτάμενος μεγάροισι
τεθνάμεν ἢ τάδε γ᾽ αἰὲν ἀεικέα ἔργ᾽ ὁράασθαι

(And if I, fighting alone, were subdued by all their number,
then I would rather die, cut down in my own palace,
than have to go on watching forever these shameful
   activities. . . .)

Telemachus, put on the defensive by the stranger's strong
rebuke, defends himself by asserting that he is an only child
and his enemies are very numerous (117–25). This confron-
tation foreshadows the true nature of the reunion to come.

Father and son do not know one another, and it will take some time for them to achieve the relationship that Telemachus and Eumaios share.

The recognition is the centerpiece of the book, occupying as it does a little more than 150 lines (156–320) in the middle. It is the first recognition and, in some sense, the most important. The poet has led up to it by beginning the entire poem with the son; their reunion marks the turning point.

Magically transformed by Athena into his heroic prime, Odysseus at first is taken for a god by Telemachus (181–85), a prudent course in the ancient world when a guest suddenly changes appearance.[10] We therefore note with surprise the curt tone of Odysseus' reply (187–88).

> οὔ τίς τοι θεός εἰμι· τί μ᾿ ἀθανάτοισιν ἐΐσκεις;
> ἀλλὰ πατὴρ τεός εἰμι.

(No, I am not a god. Why liken me to the immortals?
But I am your father. . . .)

What causes this reaction? It is hardly a reasonable one under the circumstances. We are, I think, meant to realize that Odysseus is still smarting over the less than heroic first impression his son has just made on him. Furthermore, he now realizes, somewhat to his annoyance, that heroic self-presentation will not suffice. Telemachus, not at all dissuaded by the annoyed reaction, denies the stranger's claim once again (194) and politely explains to soften his opponent that no mortal could so transform himself. Odysseus rebukes him for continuing to doubt ("it ill befits you," οὔ σε ἔοικε, 202), but adds the corroborative detail that he is now home in the twentieth year (206) and explains that Athena is responsible for the transformation (207–8). Telemachus embraces him and they weep. So ends, it at first appears, the recognition

---

[10] See Kearns, "The Return of Odysseus," who makes a case for his return as a variant on the story of the visitation to mortals of a disguised god.

with no convincing proof offered. Telemachus, we may with justice think, in contrast to his father, is a bit too trusting. But the scene does not stop here; the poet continues (220–22):

καί νύ κ' ὀδυρομένοισιν ἔδυ φάος ἠελίοιο,
εἰ μὴ Τηλέμαχος προσεφώνεεν ὃν πατέρ' αἶψα·
"ποίῃ γὰρ νῦν δεῦρο, πάτερ φίλε, νηΐ

(And now the light of the sun would have set on their crying,
had not Telemachus spoken a quick word to his father:
"What kind of ship was it, father dear . . . ?")

We realize by the probing turn of phrase "with what sort of ship" (ποίῃ . . . νηΐ, used only here in Homeric verse) that Telemachus still seeks proof. His embrace was designed to disarm the stranger's annoyance. And it has worked, for Odysseus replies patiently with facts (226ff.) and then requests information about the number of the suitors (235ff.).

It is in this reply that Telemachus receives the assurance he seeks. For as Odysseus turns to the business at hand, namely planning destruction for the suitors, he remarks at line 233:

νῦν αὖ δεῦρ' ἱκόμην ὑποθημοσύνῃσιν 'Αθήνης

(But now I have come to this place by the advice of Athena.)

So has Telemachus! At the opening of the previous book the poet carefully made a point of telling us that Telemachus was awake when Athena told him to go to Eumaios' place as soon as he arrived back in Ithaca (15.4–8, 36–42 especially). In fact, each of them has been sent to Eumaios with the same words (13.404–5 = 15.38–39). Like two halves of a lovers' token the pieces fit. From this point forth Telemachus no longer doubts his father's identity, but, revealing the characteristic cautionary foresight that stamps the family, he questions in lines 241ff. his father's tactical judgment. The odds are too great, he points out, two against more than one hundred, and he ends with a peremptory challenge (256–57):

ἀλλὰ σύ γ᾽, εἰ δύνασαί τιν᾽ ἀμύντορα μερμηρίξαι,
φράζευ, ὅ κέν τις νῶϊν ἀμύνοι πρόφρονι θυμῷ.

(But you, if you can think of some ally,
someone who would protect us with a will, name him.)

(My trans.)

Odysseus throws his words back in his face (259–61):

τοιγὰρ ἐγὼν ἐρέω, σὺ δὲ σύνθεο καί μευ ἄκουσον·
καὶ φράσαι ἤ κεν νῶϊν 'Αθήνη σὺν Διὶ πατρὶ
ἀρκέσει, ἦέ τιν᾽ ἄλλον ἀμύντορα μερμηρίξω.

(So, then, I will tell you. Hear me and understand me
and consider whether Athena with Zeus father helping will be
enough for us, or whether I must think of some other helper.)

Far from being cowed, Telemachus admits that these are excellent helpers (263), but suggests that they are remote and
rather busy (264–65). Odysseus brushes this aside with a flat
assurance that they will be present when the trouble starts
and gives Telemachus his marching orders (270ff.). In his reply Telemachus makes himself a partner by suggesting an
important alteration in Odysseus' plan (311–15) and ends
with a challenge, "if truly you know a sign from aegis-bear-
ing Zeus" (320). This statement reveals that he continues to
harbor real doubts. We know that Odysseus will not let that
remark go by unanswered. And so we leave them talking,
revising their plans against the suitors, and getting to know
each other. Telemachus has shown his mettle against the
toughest debater of them all. And, if he has been a bit cheeky
and has gotten the worst of it at times, he has also held his
own and gotten the assurance that he needed.

Against this backdrop, Homer shifts the scene to Ithaca
town (321ff.) to show us the suitors richly deserving of the
destruction now being planned. Antinoos, we learn, headed
the ambush party (365–70) and, in frustration at its failure,
authors a proposal to murder Telemachus outright (371–72).
The suitors table the proposal and Penelope appears to de-

nounce them for it (409–51). She reminds Antinoos how
Odysseus once protected his father (424–30). Antinoos at
least says nothing; Eurymachos brazenly swears to protect
Telemachus and himself tells how Odysseus used to dandle
him on his knee (443–44). Homer allows himself a rare comment (448):

Ὥς φάτο θαρσύνων, τῷ δ᾽ ἤρτυεν αὐτὸς ὄλεθρον.

(So he spoke, encouraging her, but himself was planning
the murder.)

As it had opened at daybreak, the book artfully closes at
nightfall with the return of Eumaios to Telemachus and
Odysseus, who has been changed back to resemble the old
beggar. Telemachus asks after his ambushers; he smiles at
the account of their discomfiture and shares a meaningful
glance with his father (476–77). Father and son have come a
long way towards knowing one another in this one day.

Books Seventeen to Twenty

Books seventeen to twenty take place at the palace. The change of venue inexorably brings the revenge a step closer. Most crucially Homer depicts Penelope in the course of these books as gradually coming to think of Odysseus as alive. Telemachus' return, Theoklymenos' prediction of Odysseus' return, the presence of the beggar, the defeat of the suitors' minion Iros, all contribute to Penelope's new outlook—an outlook that culminates in her decision to set the contest of the bow at the close of the nineteenth book. The suitors by contrast are shown repeatedly to be as vile as possible by their abuse of the beggar as they feast and by the actions of the servants who adhere to them. The suitors not only have no regard for guests and strangers, they enjoy tormenting their inferiors.

The books are carefully structured to form an artistic group. Melanthios and Melantho, the chief helpmates of the suitors and an obvious doublet, abuse the beggar wantonly in each of these books. Note the careful *a b b a* order in which they appear: Melanthios in book 17, Melantho in 18, Melantho in 19, Melanthios in 20. Moreover, near the close of three of the four books (nineteen alone is excepted), one of the leading suitors reviles the disguised Odysseus at meal time and throws something at him. Also serving to mark these books off as a unit, Theoklymenos begins them with a prediction that Odysseus is in Ithaca (17.152ff.) and closes them with a surrealistic vision of the suitors' death (20.351ff.).

Omens, which up to now have played a small, but not insignificant, role, take on a major part in promoting the action here and in the next tetrad. They appear primarily to members of the household of Odysseus and to Odysseus himself.

They provide reassurance at critical points by indicating the favor of the gods. At the same time, the need for them (they are at times requested) suggests the critical nature of events. Homer seems to employ them in part as a narrative device to raise the level of action. The suitors' inability, moreover, to heed them and be warned portrays the extent of their delusion.

These books may well be viewed as variations on a theme: in each one Odysseus receives abuse from the suitors or their henchmen. Homer avoids monotony, however, by varying the emphasis to add much richness of detail. Seventeen has as its centerpiece the arrival of Odysseus at his palace; eighteen features Penelope beguiling gifts from the suitors as her disguised husband watches. The high point of this tetrad and one of the high points in the entire poem is the evening meeting between Odysseus and his wife in book nineteen. It is a masterpiece of subtle character-drawing. Book twenty postpones the contest of the bow in order to give us one last reprise on the theme of the evil suitors and their equally bad servants as contrasted to the loyal servant, here Philoitios. The final book of this tetrad thus slows the tempo and lowers the tension in careful preparation for the suspense-filled contest of the bow in book twenty-one, the first book of the final tetrad.

BOOK SEVENTEEN

In book seventeen the poet brings Telemachus and Odysseus to the palace to wreak, if they can, vengeance on their enemies. This and the next three books show Odysseus experiencing for himself the wanton insolence of the suitors. We take a certain grim pleasure, as we see the suitors abuse the old beggar, in our knowledge that Odysseus will indeed get his revenge. This book also begins to suggest a change in Penelope from helplessness in the face of the boorish suitors to an uncertain feeling of hope, a growing sense that something has changed that justifies action. Homer never describes Penelope as changing; rather, he shows a change and invites us from the context to understand what has prompted it.

Penelope in this book for the first time wishes Antinoos and all the suitors dead (494–500). On the surface, Antinoos' striking of the beggar triggers her prayer. Though she may well be shocked by the mistreatment of the beggar, the strength of her hatred is clearly prompted by the whole situation, particularly by Antinoos' actions as the ringleader in the plot to kill Telemachus. Now that Telemachus is safely home, Penelope can move from worry about Telemachus to wishing actively for the death of the suitors. Telemachus' report to Penelope, which includes Menelaos' wish that Odysseus would return and kill the suitors (132–37) and Proteus' report that Odysseus is alive with Calypso (140–46), followed by Theoklymenos' prophecy that Odysseus is already in Ithaca (157), certainly aids this mood.[1]

This book has a clear structure. The central section deals with Odysseus' arrival at the palace and his initial reception by the suitors (166–491). It is framed by lines that portray Penelope. In each case she hears a prediction of Odysseus' return and wishes that it would happen (157–65, 525–40). In each, moreover, she makes a request to hear news of Odysseus and is at first rebuffed (44–51, 544–73), in the first part by Telemachus and in the last by Odysseus. The next book reveals a similar framing structure with Penelope now in the center and Odysseus at the edges.

When Telemachus arrives back at the palace, the women fuss over him and treat him like a little boy (31–35). They try, as it were, to retie the apron strings; they do not yet perceive that he has changed. Penelope comes down to hear the news of his trip. Emblematic of his growth, Telemachus realizes that he must first go to the assembly to see to his guest (52–

---

[1] On the change in Penelope, see also Murnaghan, *Disguise and Recognition in the "Odyssey,"* 46–52.

56) and dismisses his mother almost irritably (46–51). Note that Penelope does as she is told (58–60), except that instead of remaining upstairs as we have come to expect, she returns, for she is present in the scene that follows (99–165). This uncharacteristic behavior marks a change and underlines her eagerness to hear not the news of his journey, as she had at first claimed, but now, as she more candidly expresses it in her petulance, what Telemachus has learned of Odysseus (101–6). At the assembly Telemachus' actions reinforce our sense of his growing maturity—he avoids the suitors but meets with the elders (66–70) and confides in them before he recounts his news to Penelope. They as the representatives of the community appropriately hear the news first. He further signals his independence by openly indicating his intention to retaliate against the suitors if he can (82).

Odysseus now comes to the palace guided by the old swineherd (182–323). In keeping with his journeys in the poem, this journey too, albeit in passing, has dark, otherworldly elements. It takes place as evening comes on (191); they encounter on the path a darkling creature, Melanthios,[2] and find at the entrance to the palace a dog. Melanthios, the first minion of the suitors whom Odysseus encounters, presages their insolence. He curses the two old men without provocation (215–32), kicks the old beggar (233–34), and wishes Telemachus dead (251–53). He is a thoroughly evil creature and it is not without meaning that he and Eurymachos are especially close (257). Odysseus contemplates retaliating for the kick by killing him (235–37), but here exercises a restraint that he will need in full measure in dealing with the suitors.

The encounter with his faithful old dog Argos (290–327) is not only a very moving scene, it depicts Odysseus at the cru-

---

[2] His name and, of course, the name of his female counterpart Melantho derive from the word *melas*, which means "black." He could well be named "Blackie" in English.

cial moment when he enters his palace for the first time in twenty years as a loving master and vividly reminds the audience of his rightful place as lord of the manor. There could not be a better symbol of the abuse of Odysseus' house and most valued personal possessions than the decrepit, neglected state of this once magnificent beast. He is visible proof of what the suitors are doing to Odysseus' possessions. Most of all, the Argos episode adds a note of danger, for it shows that Odysseus' disguise can be penetrated, in fact has been before he even crosses the threshold!

Odysseus now enters the palace. Homer fixes the moment visually for us with several lines of description (339–41):

ἷζε δ᾽ ἐπὶ μελίνου οὐδοῦ ἔντοσθε θυράων,
κλινάμενος σταθμῷ κυπαρισσίνῳ ὅν ποτε τέκτων
ξέσσεν ἐπισταμένως καὶ ἐπὶ στάθμην ἴθυνε.

(He sat down then on the ashwood threshold, inside the
   doorway,
leaning against the doorpost of cypress wood, which the
   carpenter
once had expertly planed, and drawn it true to a chalkline.)

These lines convey the basic solidity of the house and fittingly frame its master. Telemachus as host greets the beggar with handsome portions of food (343–45). Antinoos here is shown in a particularly odious light. Parallel to Melanthios he abuses Eumaios (375–79), is stingy even with another's food (455–57), and finally hits the beggar with a footstool (462). He flouts Telemachus and every rule of hospitality. His actions bring a rejoinder from Odysseus that Antinoos may die if there are any gods who protect beggars (475–76). Even Antinoos' fellow suitors are scandalized by his behavior and rebuke him (483–87). This beggar has quickly breached, if only temporarily, their united front. Up to now Antinoos as ringleader has had their complete support. The situation is changing, we realize, and the realization sensitizes us to Penelope's growing awareness of the same thing. The book closes with a short but very important view of Penelope (492–606). On hearing that the beggar has been struck she utters a seemingly spontaneous wish aimed at Antinoos (494): "Just so may Apollo, the glorious archer, strike you down." This mention of Apollo coming first from her lips anticipates, we come to realize, her impulse later this same day (at the close of the nineteenth book) to set the contest of the bow, Apollo's weapon, for the morrow, Apollo's feast day. A few lines later Telemachus sneezes just after she has wished that Odysseus might come home and punish the suitors (539–40). Penelope cautiously, so the wistful "may it happen" (γένοιτο) of line 546 suggests, takes it as an omen for the death of the suitors. She cannot allow herself too much hope. Still, she sends Eumaios to summon the beggar so she can hear for herself what he has to report about Odysseus. Instead of immediately answering the queen's summons, astonishingly—and Penelope is astonished (576)—this beggar very sensibly, as Penelope (586) and Eumaios (580) both realize, suggests that a private meeting in the evening after the suitors have left for the night is preferable. Whatever else, Penelope clearly recognizes that there is something special about this beggar. He does not behave like an ordinary beggar, who would come immediately on being summoned by the queen, and he displays unusual prudence. As "most sensible" (περίφρων, 585) Penelope observes, he thinks "sensibly" (οὐκ ἄφρων, 586). The juxtaposition of these words in successive lines is meaningful.

This book depicts the beginnings of a change for the better in the fortunes of Odysseus' supporters at the palace. The prediction by Theoklymenos near the beginning and Telemachus' sneeze near the close, the frequent wish expressed by almost every character in the book that Odysseus' enemies come to an evil end, the arrival of the beggar, the rift among the suitors, Penelope's explicit wish for the death of Anti-

noos, and the unusual behavior of the beggar all contribute
to a growing sense that the balance is shifting. The gain is
subtly conveyed because, on the surface of it, Odysseus has
placed himself in a very precarious position and has, as yet,
found no means to extricate himself. Clearly he pins great
hopes on his meeting with the queen. The audience with its
superior knowledge, of course, sees with pleasure the tables
being turned on the suitors; Penelope, an actor in the unfolding story, also seems to sense it. The suitors are now not the
only ones who can plan or wish for another's death. Elements beyond their control at last are at work.

BOOK EIGHTEEN

Practically the last thing we had seen in book seventeen was
Odysseus, the beggar, declining Penelope's request for an interview there and then. Rather he proposed that they not
meet until after sundown. In the final lines of that book
Homer then strongly depicted the approach of evening. The
emphatic juxtaposition of "dusk having come on" (δειελιή-
σας, the last word of line 599 in book seventeen) with "at
dawn" (ἠῶθεν, the first word of line 600) specifically points to
a time late in the day. The effect is carefully reinforced by the
final words of the seventeenth book: "For now evening
(δείελον ἦμαρ) had come on." With these words the poet
deliberately leads his audience to expect that interview to occur next. But the face-to-face meeting between the disguised
hero and his wife, who have not been together alone in
twenty years, is a great moment, not to be squandered, but
rather to be deployed to greatest effect. It will be a high point
of this part of the poem and indeed a crucial point in the
entire story. Moreover, the delicacy of the situation, the potential for discovery will in the telling grip the hearer. With
sure storyteller's instinct, Homer now postpones the meeting
for an entire book, forcing us to hold our expectations in
abeyance.

By doing this he has created a difficult practical problem for himself: he must come up with something good as a substitute or risk losing his audience's interest. Homer does not disappoint. He offers us first the fast moving mock-epic battle of the beggars and then a memorable view of Penelope, the object of so much attention.

Eighteen is a very carefully crafted book that falls roughly into thirds of about 150 lines each. The structure emphasizes Penelope by placing her in the center. The sections on each side portray Odysseus dealing with the suitors. In the first (1–157), he defeats Iros; in the last (304–428), he must bear the insult of having a stool thrown at him. The two sections reveal a similar organization. Each falls into two parts. In the first part of each section Odysseus is abused by a follower of the suitors (Iros, Melantho), deals with one of the ringleaders (Antinoos, Eurymachos), and gets the better of them. In the second part Amphinomos behaves in a civilized manner (120–57, 412–28).

The duel between the beggar Iros and the disguised Odysseus is most memorable. The spectacle of the two beggars fighting on the stoop has natural comic potential. While Homer does not ignore the humor, he emphasizes the ugly aspects, using the scene to underscore the brutality of the suitors. Iros, as a hanger-on of the suitors, characterizes them, and his defeat foreshadows theirs.[3] He is a bully and, like many bullies, a coward at heart. When faced with a real fight, he shivers with fear and must be forced to fight (75–77). The suitors with Antinoos as spokesman take savage pleasure in his discomfiture and threaten horrible punishments should he lose (83–87). When he is felled like a dead animal (98), they laugh cruelly (100). The phrase used brilliantly encapsulates the fatally ironic import of events for the suitors—"they died with laughter" (γέλῳ ἔκθανον).

---

[3] Levine, "*Odyssey* 18: Iros as Paradigm for the Suitors."

The humor of the scene lies primarily in the mock-epic style in which it is told. Overtones of single warriors meeting in deadly combat are heard. The introduction of Iros well illustrates the manner (1–9).

Ἦλθε δ᾽ ἐπὶ πτωχὸς πανδήμιος, ὃς κατὰ ἄστυ
πτωχεύεσκ᾽ Ἰθάκης, μετὰ δ᾽ ἔπρεπε γαστέρι μάργῃ
ἀζηχὲς φαγέμεν καὶ πιέμεν· οὐδέ οἱ ἦν ἲς
οὐδὲ βίη, εἶδος δὲ μάλα μέγας ἦν ὁράασθαι.
Ἀρναῖος δ᾽ ὄνομ᾽ ἔσκε· τὸ γὰρ θέτο πότνια μήτηρ
ἐκ γενετῆς· Ἶρον δὲ νέοι κίκλησκον ἅπαντες,
οὕνεκ᾽ ἀπαγγέλλεσκε κιών, ὅτε πού τις ἀνώγοι·
ὅς ῥ᾽ ἐλθὼν Ὀδυσῆα διώκετο οἷο δόμοιο,
καί μιν νεικείων ἔπεα πτερόεντα προσηύδα·

(And now there arrived a public beggar, who used to go begging
through the town of Ithaca, known to fame for his ravenous
   belly
and appetite for eating and drinking. There was no real strength
in him, nor any force, but his build was big to look at.
He had the name Arnaios, for thus the lady his mother
called him from birth, but all the young men used to call him
   Iros,
because he would run and give messages when anyone told
   him.
This man had come to chase Odysseus out of his own house
and now he spoke, insulting him, and addressed him in winged
   words.)

Iros' name is postponed; his feats (begging) and appearance (large) are described first. This is the style usually reserved for famous persons and heroes. We are then not only given his name but the origin of his nickname, a device normally calculated to build up a character, but here used to add ironic humor. That he should be named for the young, beautiful, and graceful messenger of the gods tells us how we are to picture him. Clearly he epitomizes, if anyone does, the opposite of these characteristics.

Amphinomos (119ff.) provides the narrative bridge to Penelope. His courteous treatment of the beggar changes the mood somewhat. Odysseus responds by trying to warn him to leave, but in vain; "Athena bound him to be overwhelmed by the hands and spear of Telemachus" (155–56). This mention of Athena unobtrusively serves as the transition and carries us on. Homer does not waste time or make apologies to his audience, but he does offer signposts, as it were, to guide them. This is one. Without more ado, the Penelope passage begins (158–59):

Τῇ δ᾿ ἄρ᾿ ἐπὶ φρεσὶ θῆκε θεὰ γλαυκῶπις ᾿Αθήνη,
κούρῃ ᾿Ικαρίοιο, περίφρονι Πηνελοπείῃ

(But now the goddess, gray-eyed Athena, put it in the mind
of the daughter of Ikarios, circumspect Penelope. . . .)

In this central episode Homer delineates a new side of Penelope in preparation for the meeting with her disguised husband in the next book.[4] Up to this point in the poem Penelope is familiar as the lonely, bereaved wife, the overprotective, worried mother, and the isolated, nearly besieged, queen. Here for the first time we see her as an enchanting beauty, object of all men's desires (212–13). She becomes a younger, more beautiful Penelope. Homer employs by now familiar images of death and rebirth to achieve this, namely sleep (188) and reawakening (199–200), bathing (here rejected at lines 178–79) and physical transformation (195). Athena drifts a deep sleep over her, a sleep that Penelope herself likens to death (201–3), and then makes her "taller and thicker to look upon" (195). This phrase, or a close variant, is used twice before in the poem (at 6.230 and 8.20) and will occur twice afterwards (at 23.157 and 24.369). In all but the last instance, where it is used of Laertes, the phrase refers to Odysseus, and in all cases, including the present one, the context

---

[4] On this episode, see Fenik, Studies in the "Odyssey," 116–20, and Byre, "Penelope and the Suitors before Odysseus."

is one of rejuvenation. Here the attractiveness that Penelope takes on not only beguiles the men, it symbolizes a new attractiveness that life holds for her. She is somehow reborn in spirit. Not accidentally, she now thinks of Odysseus, very vividly recalling the last time she saw him and quoting verbatim his last words to her (259–70). The tension between the message in the words and the emotion that calls them forth is nicely calculated. The words repeat Odysseus' instructions to remarry when their son reached maturity and thus, on the surface, explain her act of now sanctioning the active courting process through the solicitation of presents from the suitors.[5] The direct quotation, however, depicts how immediate Odysseus is to her mind's eye. Her thoughts focus on him, just at the moment when she claims to be resigned to take a new husband.[6]

Penelope is the accomplished coquette with the suitors. She parries their compliments about her beauty with denials and, at the same time, she uses her physical attractions to elicit gifts from them (245–303), although she has no desire to marry any one of them and has in fact just shortly before acceded to Telemachus' wish that they be killed (235–38). Spice is added for the audience because she practices her coquetry in front of her husband. By using it she acquires some property and grows in her husband's eyes. He enjoys her trick (281–83). What other reaction could we expect of the master trickster in the poem? This is not the last time that we shall have occasion to observe that husband and wife are much alike.

[5] By showing Penelope as acting in response to the specific instructions of her husband, the poet portrays her as behaving in an entirely proper manner. Furthermore, the timing of this agreement to allow herself to be courted, the late afternoon of the day before the slaughter, explicitly characterizes the suitors' prior attempts as improper and done without the lady's approval.

[6] Van Nortwick, "Penelope and Nausicaa," draws a parallel between Penelope's confused emotions in books eighteen and nineteen and those of Nausicaa in book six.

As Antinoos had been put in a bad light in the first section by being coupled with Iros, so here at the end Eurymachos is coupled with Melantho. Not only do they use the same abusive words to scold the beggar (331–33 = 391–93), they sleep together (325). Eurymachos' disdain for Penelope and the house of Odysseus could not be clearer. He compounds his guilt by throwing, as Antinoos had in the previous book (17.462), a footstool at Odysseus (394–97). The two ringleaders mark themselves. Homer equates them and uses them with care.

The book closes quietly. Amphinomos, again used to make the transition, restores order by proposing that they make a libation and then retire to their homes (419). This action is his raison d'être. Homer wants the suitors out of the palace so as to establish the correct (i.e., private) atmosphere for the evening interview between Penelope and the beggar.

B O O K   N I N E T E E N

The first fifty-two lines of book nineteen form a very important self-contained introduction; the repetition of lines 1 and 2 as lines 51 and 52 clearly sets it off. In it Odysseus and Telemachus take advantage of the departure of the suitors for the night to remove the arms from the hall.[7] This act both prepares practically for the destruction of the suitors and creates an appropriate setting, a mood of conspiracy if you will, for the critical decision of Penelope to set the contest of the bow for the next day. This she does at the end of the long interview between herself and the beggar, which takes up most of this book. The nineteenth book as a whole, then, moves events forward materially towards their conclusion. Light plays an important role in these initial lines. As Telemachus and his father perform this first act leading to the

[7] For a discussion of the other passages in the poem where the removal is mentioned, see Goold, "The Removal of the Arms."

slaughter, Athena lights the way for them with an unusually powerful lamp (34–40). The gods and light, namely victory, attend them. Light and fire in this poem, as in the *Iliad*, accompany the victors.[8] The symbolic meaning of Athena's act is clear.

Homer also uses these lines to reintroduce a character who has a crucial role to play in the denouement, namely Eurykleia. Summoned by Telemachus to shut the women in their quarters (15–17), she senses that something is up and asks the leading question (24), "What woman following along then will bear a light for you?" Her question points out that he will need aid of a certain kind if he is to succeed. She is clearly volunteering and wants to be taken into his confidence. Who would be more appropriate? After all, she lighted his way to bed and tucked him in at the end of book one (428–42). In the second book (354–80) he came to her for help and confided in her about his journey. And she was the first to greet him on his return to the palace (17.31). Her special concern for Telemachus is clear throughout. Given all this, his response comes as an abrupt surprise (27–28):

ξεῖνος ὅδ᾽· οὐ γὰρ ἀεργὸν ἀνέξομαι ὅς κεν ἐμῆς γε
χοίνικος ἅπτηται, καὶ τηλόθεν εἰληλουθώς.

(This stranger will. I will not suffer a man who feeds from
our stores, and does not work, even though he comes from far
off.)

It is obviously an excuse to put her off. Carrying a lamp is not ordinarily man's work in Homeric poetry. The rebuff is made more acute by the fact that Telemachus has clearly taken the old beggar into his confidence. Even so, Eurykleia obeys and locks the doors of the great hall (30). The tension in this brief encounter neatly prepares for the accidental recognition of Odysseus by Eurykleia later in the book (392ff.). Given the advice that Odysseus has received from Agamem-

---

[8] Whitman, *Homer and the Heroic Tradition*, 128–53, esp. 129–44.

non in the underworld (11.427–28, 441–43, and especially 455–56) and from Athena just after reaching Ithaca (13.307–10, 333–36), he is understandably reluctant to reveal himself to anyone unnecessarily; thus Telemachus must put Eurykleia off here. Nevertheless, the function she performs of keeping the maidservants out of the way will again be required when the suitors are being killed. The accidental recognition achieves what is needed and, I shall suggest below, adds something special in its own context.

Telemachus has helped his father store away the armor; it is now up to Odysseus to achieve what he can with Penelope. He still has no clearly defined plan for killing the suitors (52). Now begins the long-awaited interview.[9] Within the limitations imposed by the customs of the time, Homer has created the most intimate setting possible. It is quite late at night; the suitors have gone. The serving women quietly cleaning up after the feast (61–64) provide the indistinct background against which this all but private tête-à-tête occurs. Homer now uses Melantho (65–95) to add a new note, to portray a unanimity of feeling in these two people who are, at least outwardly, strangers. Each rebukes Melantho harshly and threatens her with punishment for her behavior (83–88, 91–92). From the start, then, a sense of intimacy informs the interview.

The queen begins conventionally enough (105):

τίς πόθεν εἰς ἀνδρῶν; πόθι τοι πόλις ἠδὲ τοκῆες;

(What man are you and whence? Where is your city? Your parents?)

Odysseus does not answer her question; instead, he observes fulsomely that her fame, like that of a blameless king in the flowering of his rule, reaches up to wide heaven (107–14). Outside of the fact that it might be judicious flattery, what

---

[9] See also Austin, *Archery at the Dark of the Moon*, 214–32 for a nice examination of this encounter.

can he intend? The comparison could not be further from the truth. Penelope's situation is exactly the opposite of the picture given by his words. Her domain lacks a king and hardly prospers; her son's life is in danger. Odysseus then begs off telling about himself because it is too sad a tale; his mourning would be a nuisance, "since it is quite a tiresome thing to mourn unendingly" (120). Surely he means to provoke her by reminding her of the prosperity that she should enjoy but does not and to put her on the defensive by suggesting that weeping is not an adequate response.

It works. Penelope responds with a very personal account of her predicament and what she has tried to do about it (124–63). She speaks in the first person throughout. Obviously Homer is not out to portray her as a talkative woman who tells her troubles to every stranger who happens along. Rather, he means us to understand, the picture of the king in lines 109–14 has vividly reminded her of Odysseus and what life was like for them before he left for Troy. The first three lines of her reply (124–26), otherwise most perplexing, then become perfectly comprehensible, for she speaks of the loss of her physical beauty once her husband, Odysseus, had departed for Troy. She ends her account by saying that she has run out of plans (157–58). The note is plaintive. Odysseus has made much progress in this first exchange, for she all but asks for his advice. She stops herself short of that, however, and repeats her request to know who he is (162–63).

The unique phrase "from a fabled oak or a rock" in line 163 puzzles until we realize that it is meant to recall a similar unique phrase in the *Iliad* and, with it, one of the *Iliad's* most poignant moments—the memorable soliloquy that Hector delivers in lines 99–130 of the twenty-second book, as Achilles, burning like the dog star, races across the field toward him. Hector desperately tries to find a way out, but soon realizes that he must face him, that it is too late to strike a bargain, and that words will avail him nothing, words such as young lovers whisper to each other "from an oak or a rock"

(126). Without mentioning Andromache, the image expresses Hector's feelings for her and his sadness at the loss. This reminder heightens the tragedy of his imminent death. Here in the *Odyssey* the words encapsulate the strong emotions that Odysseus has tapped, for they point to Penelope's fond thoughts of her past love and her sense of her own tragic loss of that love.[10]

In answer to her request to know who he is, Odysseus identifies himself as a Cretan, as she already has heard from Eumaios (17.523). He gives her a good deal of circumstantial detail about Crete (172–78) and little information about himself beyond a royal lineage (178–80). She is a queen; he, therefore, makes himself a prince, younger brother of Idomeneus, famed like Odysseus for his exploits at Troy. The name he chooses for himself, Aithon (The Blazing One), sustains the fire imagery of the opening scene of the book. The mention of Idomeneus (181) leads naturally to Odysseus, and he devotes almost half his speech to describing how he entertained Odysseus on his way to Troy (185–202).

We have seen how emotionally Penelope reacted to the oblique reminder of Odysseus, so we expect here a strong reaction to this detailed account of her husband's activities. Homer does not disappoint. He devotes to it one of his finest similes (205–9):

> ὡς δὲ χιὼν κατατήκετ᾽ ἐν ἀκροπόλοισιν ὄρεσσιν,
> ἥν τ᾽ Εὖρος κατέτηξεν, ἐπὴν Ζέφυρος καταχεύῃ·
> τηκομένης δ᾽ ἄρα τῆς ποταμοὶ πλήθουσι ῥέοντες·
> ὡς τῆς τήκετο καλὰ παρήϊα δάκρυ χεούσης,
> κλαιούσης ἑὸν ἄνδρα παρήμενον.

[10] The fact that the *Odyssey* poet is aware of and refers to the *Iliad* is well known; see, for example, Griffin, *Homer, The "Odyssey,"* 63–70. To what degree Homeric poetry refers to a particular text or to the well-developed tradition is a matter for discussion. For the generally accepted view that it is the tradition to which it refers, see Nagy, *The Best of the Achaeans*, 42–43. Pucci's recent study, *Odysseus Polutropos*, takes this position as its starting point.

(As the snow melts along the high places of the mountains
when the West Wind has piled it there, but the South Wind
    melts it,
and as it melts the rivers run full flood. It was even
so that her beautiful cheeks were streaming tears, as Penelope
wept for her man, who was sitting there by her side. . . .)

This is a weeping such as only a hero can receive. Need one
call attention to the delicate rightness of snow white for the
lady's skin, or the exquisite contrast of settings between the
outdoor vista of the snowcapped mountain with its streams
and the indoor close-up of a weeping woman sitting near the
fire? Each gains by contemplation of the other, so completely
do the images complement one another. At length Penelope
seeks proof, a description of Odysseus' clothing and companions. This is just what he had hoped for. Now he can
warm to his task and speak of Odysseus without pretending
not to. With appropriate protestations (221–23, 236–40), he
describes himself and the clothing he wore twenty years before in elaborate detail (225–43).

The method in his approach is clear. By reminding Penelope of Odysseus more explicitly and more concretely in each
successive speech, he clearly plans to gain her confidence,
and thus her aid, without openly revealing his identity to
her. So far his strategy has worked beautifully. What he has
not counted on, however, although forewarned by Eumaios,
is the degree to which she has become discouraged by the
passage of time and the many times her hopes have been
raised only to be dashed. He is hardly the first wanderer to
claim he has news of Odysseus (14.122–30). She has reached
the point where she can not allow herself the luxury of hope.
The sure signs that he has given do offer hope. Weeping she
acknowledges the signs (255–57), but concludes with pessimistic finality, "I will never again welcome him home" (257–
58).

Not recognizing her reaction for what it is, Odysseus now

plays his trump card. He alludes to their lovemaking (266), bids her not to weep, and assures her that Odysseus will be home very soon. Presumably to be more persuasive, he provides a rather specific account of his wanderings (273–86), so specific in fact that he must catch himself at line 287 with the lame "so Pheidon King of the Thesprotians told me." After adding some details about a trip to Dodona, he ends by reiterating that Odysseus is very close by and swears an oath that he will be here during this very *lykabas* (306). Despite the controversy about the meaning of the word, it is clear that Homer glosses it in the next line (307) as the period at the waning of one month and the rising of the next. This is logically the daylight period preceding the rising of the new moon. He thus swears to Odysseus' return during a specific period of daylight, presumably tomorrow. He could not be more definite; his purpose is to encourage her to act now.

But Penelope cannot afford the hope that he proffers, so she responds by confirming her conviction that Odysseus will not come home ever (313). She then, in a move designed to terminate the interview, orders her handmaidens to bathe him and make up a bed for him (317–18). Odysseus now faces a moment of crisis. The interview has not gone according to plan; he has not achieved what he wanted. In fact, he has not accomplished much of anything, so he must try to prolong it at all costs. Simple agreement with her suggestion will terminate the interview at once. He therefore counters in the most reasonable way possible by saying he has no need of fancy coverlets nor footbasins and washings by women such as these maidservants, but if there is some old and virtuous woman he would not mind such a one touching his feet (336–48). Odysseus makes a calculated gamble here, for his words clearly point to Eurykleia. Scar or no—and Homer does make Odysseus forget about it—his old nurse knows him as intimately as his mother. To ensure Penelope's presence for a while longer, Homer here depicts Odysseus as willing to risk close contact with *the* person who is most likely to penetrate his disguise. The opening lines of the book do not allow us to suppose he does not think of Eurykleia; and the Argos episode (17.290–327) has provided ample warning that his disguise is not foolproof.

His attempt to gain Penelope's confidence by telling her about Odysseus has hit a stone wall; now, driven by necessity, though he has not spoken about Odysseus, he clearly has spoken *like* him. Penelope instinctively responds, as she had once before to this man's uncommon good sense (17.586), and speaks very warmly (350–52):

> ξεῖνε φίλ᾽· οὐ γάρ πώ τις ἀνὴρ πεπνυμένος ὧδε
> ξείνων τηλεδαπῶν φιλίων ἐμὸν ἵκετο δῶμα,
> ὡς σὺ μάλ᾽ εὐφραδέως πεπνυμένα πάντ᾽ ἀγορεύεις·

(Dear friend, never before has there been any man so thoughtful among those friends from far places who have come to my palace
as guests, so thoughtful and so well-considered is everything you say.)

The repetition of "dear friend," "a friend more dear" (φίλ᾽, φιλίων) in lines 350 and 351 is particularly notable. In addition, the word order in line 358, νίψον σοῖο ἄνακτος ὁμήλικα ("Wash of your master the agemate"), teases us for a brief moment into thinking that she has recognized him and naturally introduces a statement that reveals the extraordinary change that has occurred in her thinking about Odysseus during this exchange (358–59):

> καί που Ὀδυσσεὺς
> ἤδη τοιόσδ᾽ ἐστὶ πόδας τοιόσδε τε χεῖρας·

(Perhaps Odysseus
is by now also like this man, his feet and hands.)   (My trans.)

The present tense is all-important; far from dead, she here thinks of him as alive and growing old (360). The footwashing now takes place (361–505) as Penelope sits by, absorbed in her thoughts of Odysseus.

Penelope's revived hope that Odysseus lives thus provides the backdrop for the account of his birth and his greatest exploit as a boy. Such an account is integral to establishing fully his identity. Eurykleia, the person who had placed him on his grandfather's knees soon after his birth (401) and the person who gave him suck (482–83), takes the place of his mother. The similarity between their names, Antikleia-Eurykleia, is hardly fortuitous. In short, Odysseus experiences a necessary reunion with a mother figure, without which his identity would be incomplete. Here then we are given the story of his naming by his mother's father, Autolykos. The stress on his name meaning angry (407–9) underlines his attitude toward the suitors.[11] The scar also receives here the emphasis it needs to give Odysseus a means of quickly identifying himself in the coming emergency. The aura of nostalgic recollection created by this unusually long flashback does much to shape our understanding of Penelope's frame of mind at this point in the evening. For her, as for us, Odysseus has become a little more alive.

We are not surprised to find at the end of the flashback that Penelope now wants to go on talking with the beggar. She seeks his advice (525–34) and asks him in particular to interpret her dream in which an eagle comes from the mountain and kills her pet geese, all twenty of them. The eagle in the dream then says that he is her husband and the geese are the suitors whom he will kill (535–50). This dream of course needs no interpretation, and Odysseus duly repeats that it portends the destruction of the suitors. Imperceptibly Penelope has come to confide in him.[12] Even though she now denies the dream categorically as a false one (560–69), she has,

<hr>

[11] See Dimock's well-known article, "The Name of Odysseus."

[12] Amory, "The Reunion of Odysseus and Penelope," suggests that Penelope here intuitively realizes that the stranger is her husband; see esp. pp. 105–6.

by recounting it, informed him of this very important portent.[13] Now she proposes to set the contest of the bow for tomorrow (572–81), again carefully looking to the beggar for his reaction. He encourages her, affirming that Odysseus will be home before any of the suitors can string the bow (584–87). She then goes to bed weeping for Odysseus until Athena casts sweet sleep over her eyes.

The contest of the bow provides Odysseus with the opportunity he needs to implement the destruction of the suitors. Penelope comes up with it of her own accord. What makes her fasten on it? The needs of the story of course. But that is no answer. How has Homer motivated it and made it acceptable? When the suggestion comes, it seems natural. Contests are a normal way to settle upon a husband for a royal lady. Our awareness that Penelope thinks much about Odysseus in this book and the nostalgic sense created by the flashback to Odysseus' youth help in this regard. The shooting of the arrow through the axes was a special feat peculiar to Odysseus, or at least something that he did often (573–75). It is quite natural, therefore, that she should now think of it. In addition, tomorrow is Apollo's festival day; Penelope has herself called on Apollo, the archer, to kill Antinoos (17.494). She has heard, moreover, the prediction that Odysseus will be home tomorrow. What better day to set the contest of the bow? What better way to call forth Odysseus than to set a contest that requires stringing his special bow and reduplicating his special shot?

[13] She uses the motif of the gates of horn and ivory, through the first of which come true dreams and the second false ones, to deny the dream. Vergil made these gates at the end of the sixth book of his *Aeneid* a pregnant symbol, one that continues to puzzle scholars. The use here in the *Odyssey* is far simpler; it has the aura of a common way of talking about dreams, a folk motif that Penelope can employ, now that she has conveyed the information she wishes to convey, as a convenient device to dismiss the dream. As Russo suggests ("Interview and Aftermath," 10 n. 13), Homer may well have originated this elaboration of the gates of dreams for this spot in his tale. For more on these gates, see Amory, "The Gates of Horn and Ivory."

B O O K   T W E N T Y

Book twenty sets the stage for the contest and slaughter by bringing together all of the persons who are directly involved. It quite deliberately slows the pace by putting off the contest. Homer employs the natural rhythm of daylight coming with attendant preparations of a feast to motivate the action. The first 121 lines bring us to daybreak. Lines 122–239 cover morning preparations for the feast, particularly servants arriving from the estate with animals. The last section (240–394) recounts the feast, presumably at or near midday. In each of the three parts the guilt of those disloyal to Odysseus is stressed in preparation for their deaths. The serving maids sleep with the suitors (6–8); Melanthios reviles Odysseus (173–82); the suitors continue to plot Telemachus' death (241–42) and to abuse the beggar (292–300). Omens sent from Zeus in the first section and Theoklymenos' prophecy in the last reveal that the gods sanction Odysseus' vengeance.

The first part portrays the reactions of Odysseus and Penelope to the decision to set the contest of the bow. Both are agitated as the critical moment approaches. Odysseus tosses and turns, worrying about how to deal with the suitors and their families (28–43), until Athena reassures him and puts him to sleep. Penelope has had a more personal reaction; she has dreamt very vividly of Odysseus lying beside her (88–90), and she prays to Artemis to die rather than marry someone else. She naturally has strong regrets about the coming contest, which will presumably oblige her to do just that. Are we meant to wonder whether she will actually go through with it? Hearing her voice, Odysseus thinks that she has recognized him (94). Does he doubt her ability to keep his identity a secret? The poet does not specify. Rather, he simply portrays Odysseus as deeply concerned. Odysseus' formal prayer to Zeus—the use of the oxhide as a prayer rug (96–97) is unique in Homer—suggests his fundamental need for reassurance. The two omens that follow (102–19) put aside all doubts.[14]

The second section introduces the loyal cowherd, Philoi-tios. Aside from the fact that he will have a small practical role to play in the slaughter, Homer introduces him at this juncture to damn by contrast. He and Eumaios, it ought to be noticed, receive emphasis in the books set on Ithaca prior to the slaughter and forcefully put the lie to those disloyal to Odysseus, by making it clear that it was possible to remain loyal. Moved by Philoitios' strong devotion, particularly to Telemachus (214–20), Odysseus all but tells him who he is. He says in so many words that Odysseus will kill the suitors this day (232–34).

ἦ σέθεν ἐνθάδ᾽ ἐόντος ἐλεύσεται οἴκαδ᾽ Ὀδυσσεύς·
σοῖσιν δ᾽ ὀφθαλμοῖσιν ἐπόψεαι, αἴ κ᾽ ἐθέλῃσθα,
κτεινομένους μνηστῆρας, οἳ ἐνθάδε κοιρανέουσι.

(Odysseus will come home again, while you are still here
in the house, and with your own eyes, if you desire to,
you can watch him killing the suitors, who are supreme here.)

Buoyed by the omens sent from Zeus, Odysseus now has complete confidence in the outcome of the day's events.

And now in the third part the suitors gather for the festi-val. Homer adds the exquisite detail that it is the festival of "Apollo the far darter" (ἑκατηβόλος, 278); the epithet (used only here in the *Odyssey*) recalls Apollo at the opening of the *Iliad*. There the first epithet used of Apollo is the shortened form of this epithet (ἑκηβόλος, lines 14 and 21); it is followed closely by the wrathful god turning his lethal bow on the Achaean army. The image conveyed by the epithet is hardly a good omen for the suitors. Paralleling the first section, where Odysseus requested an inside and an outside omen from Zeus, the suitors see an eagle on the left (242–43), an

[14] On these reactions of Penelope and Odysseus, see Russo, "Interview and Aftermath," 11–18.

outside omen, and hear Theoklymenos' prediction (351–57), an inside one. As she had encouraged Odysseus in the first section, here Athena befuddles the suitors (346). Penelope, too, returns at the close of the book. While Odysseus and Telemachus bide their time (385–86), Penelope has drawn her chair up next to the door of the hall and overhears all that passes within (387–89). This act is unique for Penelope; she is not elsewhere an eavesdropper. Homer, of course, needs her present to fetch the bow; but the gesture suggests that she is taking an active part as an accomplice. With Theoklymenos' prophecy of death for the suitors fresh in her ears, she fetches the bow at the opening of book twenty-one.

Homer carefully uses images of fire and light and their opposites in this book to suggest victory and defeat. The day of Apollo's festival dawns (91) and Odysseus prays for a favorable omen. Zeus at once thunders from "dazzling Olympos" (103). The formula occurs only here in the *Odyssey*. The women then kindle the fire on the hearth (123), a fire that the suitors will try in vain to usurp in the next book to make the bow pliant. On the other side and associated with the suitors, Melanthios, the darkling one, reviles Odysseus (173). Theoklymenos, in his eerie vision of the suitors' fate, sees them shrouded in darkness (351–52); the sun has perished for them (356–57).

Theoklymenos' sudden departure at the close of this book (371–72) seals the suitors' doom. His leaving, juxtaposed with Penelope's rather abrupt reappearance (387–89), makes us realize that all is in readiness for the killing of the suitors. Penelope, the person in the house most affected by their actions, is present; Theoklymenos, the only outsider in this dispute involving the house of Odysseus, has departed. All involved parties are now at hand.

CHAPTER 6

Books Twenty-One to Twenty-Four

THE FINAL FOUR books do not reveal any obvious unity of the kind that the other tetrads exhibit; rather, each book covers basically one discrete event: the contest of the bow (twenty-one), the killing of the suitors (twenty-two), the reunion of Penelope and Odysseus (twenty-three), and the reunion with Laertes and rapprochement with the families of the suitors (twenty-four). This seems calculated to convey a sense of logical progression that brings the poem to a decisive and, at the same time, leisurely conclusion.

The first and third books of this tetrad stand out as most memorable; the second, while superficially exciting, really acts as a buffer between them. The final book lacks the same thematic concentration as the others and has the feel of wrapping up some loose ends. It does this efficiently enough, but with it the poet clearly winds the poem down to its close. In fact, from the great moment of the stringing of the bow at the end of book twenty-one, the crescendo, all the rest is finely wrought diminuendo.

BOOK TWENTY-ONE

The twenty-first book begins with the bow and ends with the bow. At the opening Penelope fetches it from the storeroom where it has lain these twenty years. The last scene focuses on Odysseus as he handles the bow with loving care, strings it with ease, and shoots through the axes.[1] In between Homer artfully makes us wonder just when and how the old

[1] On this shot and the various theories about it, see Page, *Folktales in Homer's "Odyssey,"* 95–113; on technical aspects of the shot, McLeod, "The Bow and the Axes."

beggar will get his hands on the bow. He postpones the moment as long as possible and uses the interim to give us a last view of the suitors vainly attempting to string the bow by any means possible. The attempt in fact so absorbs their attention that they fail to notice the movements of their underlings. Thus Odysseus has the opportunity to reveal himself with the scar as his token (219) to Eumaios and Philoitios; he then gives them instructions (229–41), particularly the crucial order to Eumaios that he is to bring him the bow at the appointed time.

The recognitions constitute the primary thematic device to portray Odysseus as reestablishing himself in Ithaca; thus, this recognition is accorded emphasis in the structure of the narrative. The action of this book indeed pivots around the scene between Odysseus and his two loyal servants, Eumaios and Philoitios (188–244). One might usefully lay out the structure of book twenty-one as follows:

a. Penelope with the bow (1–79)
b. Eumaios carries the bow to the suitors and is rebuked (80–100)
c. Telemachus (101–39)
d. Leodes and Antinoos (140–87)
THE RECOGNITION (188–244)
d. Eurymachos and Antinoos (245–72)
c. Odysseus (273–358)
b. Eumaios carries the bow to Odysseus amidst rebukes (359–79).
[Eurykleia and Philoitios bar the hall (380–92)]
a. Odysseus with the bow (393–434).

Before the recognition, a suitor (Leodes) tries the bow unsuccessfully, and then Antinoos intercedes with a suggestion to heat it (140–87); after the recognition, a suitor (Eurymachos) attempts in vain to string the bow, and Antinoos proposes a postponement (245–72). Bracketing these scenes of the suitors' difficulties with the bow come Telemachus' attempt, in which he would have succeeded on the fourth try had Odysseus not signalled to him (101–39), and Odysseus' request to have a try (273–375). The pictures of Penelope weeping over the bow at the beginning (1–79, esp. 55–57) and of Odysseus examining the bow with minute care at the close (379–430, esp. 393–405) balance one another.[2] Both sit with the bow on their laps. Another point of similarity is the striking sound effects used in each section. The doors of the storeroom make a loud noise "like a bull" as Penelope opens them to get the bow (48–50).[3] Likewise at the end Odysseus tries the bow-string; "it sang forth beautifully in response like the voice of a swallow" (411).

Since the bow is to be the focal point of the action, Homer turns to it at once. As Penelope goes to fetch it, the poet guides our eyes with rich detail: the high staircase (5), the bent key in a strong hand (6), a beautiful key of bronze with an ivory handle (7), attendant women (8), the back chamber (8–9). When she actually arrives at the chamber, we see the oaken threshold (43) planed true and straight (44), the fitted door jambs (45), and lastly the shining doors themselves (45). The actual use of the key, the unlatching of the outer leather latch and the insertion of the key accompanied by a vigorous upward motion dislodging the bolt on the inside, leads to the noise of the doors as they open. Each step is described, and the simile of the bull bellowing underlines the moment.

These two passages rich in epithets frame lines in which Homer gives in elaborate detail the background, the geneal-

---

[2] Note also that identical language is used: as Penelope "thrust" ($\mathring{\eta}\kappa\varepsilon$) home the key (47), driving it "straight in" ($\mathring{\alpha}\nu\tau\alpha\ \tau\iota\tau\upsilon\sigma\kappa o\mu\acute{\varepsilon}\nu\eta$, 48), so Odysseus "shot" ($\mathring{\eta}\kappa\varepsilon$) the arrow (420), aiming it "straight on" ($\mathring{\alpha}\nu\tau\alpha\ \tau\iota\tau\upsilon\sigma\kappa\acute{o}\mu\varepsilon\nu o\varsigma$, 421).

[3] This sound surely suggests the pent-up power of the possessions stored within. The verbs used for the sound in successive lines, $\mathring{\alpha}\nu\acute{\varepsilon}\beta\rho\alpha\chi\varepsilon\nu$ (48) and $\mathring{\varepsilon}\beta\rho\alpha\chi\varepsilon$ (49), occur only here in the *Odyssey*, but are used in the *Iliad* notably for the crash of armor or the harsh sounds of battle. The choice is deliberate. Not only is the bow with its quiver and arrows in the storeroom, but also Odysseus' prized possessions, which he left behind when he departed for Troy. These stored-up personal possessions symbolize him and his house.

ogy as it were, of this great bow (13–41). Odysseus acquired it as a guest gift in his youth (13, 20–21). Iphitos, the giver, was later killed by another host of his, Herakles, when he was staying in Herakles' house and eating at his table, a terrible perversion of the guest/host relationship (24–30, esp. 27–28). Since the poet mentions the death of Eurytos, the father of Iphitos and previous owner of the bow (32–33), we are meant to remember that Eurytos was killed by Apollo for challenging him to an archery contest (8.226–28). Odysseus did not take this bow to Troy (38–39), but left it at home as a keepsake of a dear friend (40–41). With this lineage, the bow becomes the perfect instrument with which to show the suitors wanting and then to kill them. It comes from an earlier generation of heroes, with whom even Odysseus would not vie (8.223–24). It belongs, therefore, to a world totally foreign to the suitors; such men as they can never string such a bow, much less shoot it. Note that the possibility of their stringing it never even occurs to Odysseus. Eurytos, its first owner, offers a paradigm of the folly of challenging one's better in bowmanship. As a guest gift it is the perfect instrument to bring death to these wanton abusers of the guest/host relationship. In a way, perhaps Odysseus' killing of these men also constitutes an indirect revenge for Iphitos' treacherous murder in a guest/host situation. Lastly, what better weapon to kill these would-be destroyers of his estate than one that is part of the stored wealth of the estate?[4]

Telemachus plays an important role in getting the bow into his father's hands. Homer portrays him as a bit silly; but his silliness conceals a shrewd purpose, and so we are to realize that it is an act to allay any suspicions the suitors might have. Telemachus' first words (102–17) illustrate the point. He begins with nine lines of chatter, praising his mother like some auctioneer; note, in particular, lines 106–10:

[4] On the bow, see also Clay, *The Wrath of Athena*, 89–93.

ἀλλ᾽ ἄγετε, μνηστῆρες, ἐπεὶ τόδε φαίνετ᾽ ἄεθλον,
οἵη νῦν οὐκ ἔστι γυνὴ κατ᾽ Ἀχαιίδα γαῖαν,
οὔτε Πύλου ἱερῆς οὔτ᾽ Ἄργεος οὔτε Μυκήνης·
οὔτ᾽ αὐτῆς Ἰθάκης οὔτ᾽ ἠπείροιο μελαίνης·
καὶ δ᾽ αὐτοὶ τόδε ἴστε· τί με χρὴ μητέρος αἴνου;

(But come, you suitors, since here is a prize set out before you,
a woman; there is none like her in all the Achaian country,
neither in sacred Pylos nor Argos nor in Mykene,
nor here in Ithaca itself, nor on the dark mainland.
You yourselves also know this; then why should I praise my
    mother?)

Telemachus then proposes that he have the first try on the
grounds that, if he can string the bow, it will be a consolation
to him for his mother's departure to know that he can accomplish his father's deeds. This must be the primary meaning
of his words, for he can scarcely intend to compete directly
with the suitors for his mother and, by stringing the bow,
end the contest before it has begun.[5] Rather he here means
to establish a precedent for others outside the strict confines
of the contest to have a try. He is, in short, preparing the way
for getting the bow into his father's hands. By going first he
also asserts his authority over the bow and by almost stringing it—Odysseus had to nod him off—reveals to the hearer
how much like his father he has become. His all but successful attempt comments on the suitors' vain efforts that follow
and makes us aware with what ease Odysseus will string the
bow once he gets it in his grasp.

  Odysseus asks to try the bow only after the suitors have
accepted Antinoos' proposal to postpone the contest and af-

---

[5] See, for example, Stanford in his commentary on lines 115ff. in *The "Odyssey" of Homer*. He also sums up well the other position, which is that Telemachus is competing. There exists here surely an ambiguity of motivation
that is immediately recognizable. This is the natural tendency in Western
culture for a son to compete with his father, especially for the affections of
the mother. Telemachus does, on some level, desire to equal or even best
his father.

ter they have drunk as much as they desire (273). He thus
carefully separates his request from their actual contest. Still,
the request itself impudently asserts a place far above mere
beggar. Moreover, Antinoos' proposal to postpone the contest was surely a move to save face, for, by carrying it, he
alone avoids trying the bow. Antinoos clearly suspects that
he will have no better success than the others. The beggar's
rather cheeky request then adds, as it were, insult to injury.

As he had with Polyphemos, Odysseus "craftily" (δολο-
φρονέων, 274) relies on the effect of the wine to achieve what
he wants. Clearly he means to provoke a strong reaction. In-
toxicated, Antinoos rises to the bait; the repetitions in lines
289–92 nicely convey his drunken bluster:

> οὐκ ἀγαπᾷς ὃ ἕκηλος ὑπερφιάλοισι μεθ᾽ ἡμῖν
> δαίνυσαι, οὐδέ τι δαιτὸς ἀμέρδεαι, αὐτὰρ ἀκούεις
> μύθων ἡμετέρων καὶ ῥήσιος; οὐδέ τις ἄλλος
> ἡμετέρων μύθων ξεῖνος καὶ πτωχὸς ἀκούει.

> (Don't you love it that all at your ease you *feast*
> with us bloods and don't lack of the *feast* but *hear*
> *our stories* and talk? Nor does any other
> guest beggar *hear our stories*.) (My trans.)

Instead of directly denying the beggar a turn, Antinoos, true
to his character, prefers to make threats (305–10). Significantly, these are his last words in the poem. He accuses the
beggar of being drunk and bullies him with the same vicious
threat of emasculation, etc., that he had made to Iros (18.84–
87). He introduces his threat by reminding the beggar of how
the centaurs got drunk in the house of Peirithoos and the
terrible punishment meted out to them by the Lapiths (295–
304). In his diminished mental state Antinoos fails to see how
perfectly his exemplum recoils on himself and his friends.
They are the ones who are creating a drunken brawl at what
they hope will be a wedding in the home of a king.

Penelope, who has rebuked Antinoos before for his plan to kill Telemachus (16.418–33), now (312ff.) naturally interrupts to take the beggar's part. This intervention also portrays her continued special interest in the beggar. Her emphatic denial of the possibility of marriage between the beggar and herself calls attention to itself; note especially the repeated negatives in line 319, "since there is *no* likelihood, *none at all*" (ἐπεὶ οὐδὲ μὲν οὐδὲ ἔοικε). Doth the lady protest too much? Since Penelope cannot be present at the actual slaughter, we enjoy seeing her have the last word with Antinoos and Eurymachos before it. To Eurymachos, who injects his concern about reputation (321–29), Penelope sarcastically points out that it is rather late to be worried about that (331–33) and proposes that the beggar be given the bow (336). Penelope's assertiveness gives Telemachus the opening he needs to intervene in such a way that he seems to be helping the suitors (344–53). From their point of view he rescues them from Penelope's rebukes and countermands her order about the bow. Her words in fact allow him to assert his total authority over the bow, even to give it outright to the beggar as a gift (348–49). At this point clearly he signals to Eumaios to carry the bow to his father. He cushions the effect by directing this statement to his mother and by not ending with it. Rather he ends by sending Penelope to her room (350–53) in an attempt to divert attention from Eumaios. As Odysseus had asserted his control over the bow with his nod and caused Telemachus to pass it on to the suitors (129–35), so Telemachus here asserts his control and tries to pass it on to his father.

The diversionary tactic does not succeed, and Telemachus shrewdly adopts another line. These men enjoy bullying their underlings. Note the cruel threats they make to Eumaios to force him to put the bow back (363–64). Telemachus now pretends to be one of them. He threatens old Eumaios physically and laments his impotence at dealing with his equals (369–75). Under these feigned threats of being chased out of town and being pelted with stones, Eumaios at last gets the bow to Odysseus. The suitors meanwhile laugh at the double discomfiture of Eumaios and Telemachus (376–78). For this last moment, just as their doom is sealed, they revel in what they believe to be their superior power. How appropriate it is that Homer should make Telemachus exploit their most disagreeable characteristic at this decisive moment. Once Odysseus has the bow in his hands (379), the suitors' end is at hand.

The final scene of this book has a peculiar power. Odysseus takes a grim joy in the slaughter to come, comparing it to a feast (428) and its aftermath to song (430). The simile at lines 406–9 contributes greatly to the effect:

ὡς ὅτ᾽ ἀνὴρ φόρμιγγος ἐπιστάμενος καὶ ἀοιδῆς
ῥηϊδίως ἐτάνυσσε νέῳ περὶ κόλλοπι χορδήν,
ἅψας ἀμφοτέρωθεν ἐϋστρεφὲς ἔντερον οἰός,
ὡς ἄρ᾽ ἄτερ σπουδῆς τάνυσεν μέγα τόξον Ὀδυσσεύς.

(As when a man, who well understands the lyre and singing,
easily, holding it on either side, pulls the strongly twisted
cord of sheep's gut, so as to slip it over a new peg,
so, without any strain, Odysseus strung the great bow.)[6]

Most similes primarily use language to create their effects. This one is unique in that its every step can be acted out by the singer, and certainly that is what Homer intended. Only a singularly inept singer would fail to pluck a string when he reached lines 410–411:

[6] It is highly significant that the bow, the actual instrument of Odysseus' victory over the suitors, is compared to a lyre, a stringed instrument played by singers to accompany their song. This simile nicely completes the motif of song conferring on its subjects fame, i.e., a kind of immortality. Structurally, it does not seem to be an accident that it occupies roughly the same position in this half of the poem, namely the end of the ninth book, that Odysseus' assumption of the singer's role did in the first half, namely the beginning of the ninth book. By his prowess as a singer at the court of the Phaeacians, Odysseus assured his passage home, and by his prowess as a bowman, he now assures the success of that homecoming. The comparison is most apt. See Segal, "Kleos and Its Ironies in the Odyssey," 43–44.

δεξιτερῇ δ᾽ ἄρα χειρὶ λαβὼν πειρήσατο νευρῆς·
ἡ δ᾽ ὑπὸ καλὸν ἄεισε, χελιδόνι εἰκέλη αὐδήν.

(Then plucking it in his right hand he tested the bowstring,
and it gave him back an excellent sound like the voice of a
swallow.)

The triple underlining of the moment with the description,
the action of the performer, and the sound of the instrument
arrests the attention of the audience. It is a great moment.
We are then surprised to realize that the suitors, though they
pale at the sound (412–13), do not really perceive the mortal
danger they are in (22.24–33). They remain confident in their
numbers. They do not receive our pity; yet, the reversal of
their fortunes is so sudden, unexpected, and complete that it
takes our breath away.[7]

BOOK TWENTY-TWO

Αὐτὰρ ὁ γυμνώθη ῥακέων πολύμητις Ὀδυσσεύς,
ἆλτο δ᾽ ἐπὶ μέγαν οὐδόν, ἔχων βιὸν ἠδὲ φαρέτρην
ἰῶν ἐμπλείην, ταχέας δ᾽ ἐκχεύατ᾽ ὀϊστοὺς
αὐτοῦ πρόσθε ποδῶν

(Now resourceful Odysseus stripped his rags from him, and
sprang
up atop the great threshold, holding his bow and the quiver
filled with arrows, and scattered out the swift shafts before him
on the ground next to his feet.)

So begins the twenty-second book. It is a book of rapid action that rids the palace of the suitors and disloyal servants.
When their end comes, it comes very quickly. Paradoxically,

---

[7] Murnaghan points out (Disguise and Recognition in the "Odyssey," 11–14,
67–72) that Odysseus' presentation of himself to the suitors here and in the
opening lines of the next book is like the epiphany of a god. The suitors'
failure to recognize him fits this pattern ". . . failure to recognize a disguised
god often brings mortals to disaster . . ." (68).

by the time we reach the slaughter, the expected climax of the work, we find that it is not the climax at all. After the contest of the bow, told with all suspense, the slaughter of the suitors follows as night follows day. In point of fact this book is the least memorable of the last four. This is deliberate, for, as important to the story as the suitors are in a practical sense, the emphasis is not to be on their killing, but on the return of Odysseus to resume his roles as king, father, husband, and son. The suitors are merely an unpleasant obstacle to be cleared out of the way.

Given this, Homer invests the battle with a good deal of interest. With the help of Melanthios, the suitors do make a fight of it, and Odysseus does need Athena's aid. The battle is articulated into three parts, which we may conveniently designate the slaughter with the bow (8–125), the spear fight (126–291), and the rout and mop-up (292–389). The poet keeps the realities of the fight before us and does not let us forget the large number of men Odysseus faces. As any archer would do when outnumbered and faced with the need to shoot quickly, Odysseus spreads the arrows on the ground at the ready in front of him. When he runs out of arrows and the suitors attempt to fight back, the need for armor becomes apparent, and Telemachus goes to fetch it (101–25). In a damning characterization of the suitors' resourcefulness, it is Melanthios who almost saves the day by getting arms for twelve of them before he is seized by Philoitios and Eumaios (126–200).

When the spear fight proper begins at line 203, the poet pointedly reminds us that it is four against the remaining suitors, twelve of whom we know from the passage preceding are armed. Athena now appears disguised as Mentor (205–6). She is savagely threatened by Agelaos (213–23), who by this speech takes on Antinoos' mantle and assures that the suitors remain in a negative light. The audience cannot sympathize with them. Athena then deflects the spear casts of the suitors, which they make in two groups of six, while

Odysseus and his men in response each kill a man (266–68, 283–86). Philoitios kills Ktesippos last. His speech ironically returning Ktesippos' guest gift (287–91) formally ends this stage of the fight. The suitors are now all but weaponless and in complete disarray, for Odysseus and Telemachus no longer throw their spears. Each instead uses his spear to stab one of the remaining suitors. Odysseus (293) kills Agelaos, their putative leader, and Telemachus (294) kills Leokritos, who has appeared only once before (2.242) as their spokesman. There he rebuked Mentor and suggested that Odysseus, even if he returned, would be outnumbered and killed by the suitors (2.245–51)! His death marks the end of any formal threat to Odysseus from the suitors. Immediately after it Athena waves her aegis (297) and completes the rout.

As a means of changing the mood, Homer now introduces as a pendant to the slaughter a scene (310–80) in which two characters, Leodes and Phemios, throw themselves on Odysseus' mercy. Leodes, a priest, who is known otherwise only from 21.144 and following, where he was the first to attempt to string the bow, is savagely beheaded (328–29). As one who had actively challenged Odysseus, he gets what he deserves. By contrast, the bard Phemios is saved by Telemachus, who also intercedes on behalf of Medon, the herald. Phemios and Medon are not suitors and have served the suitors only out of necessity. The mercy shown them is thus right and brings Odysseus' murderous progress to a halt. A vivid simile closes the account of the slaughter and sets it off (383–88):

τοὺς δὲ ἴδεν μάλα πάντας ἐν αἵματι καὶ κονίῃσι
πεπτεῶτας πολλούς, ὥς τ' ἰχθύας, οὕς θ' ἁλιῆες
κοῖλον ἐς αἰγιαλὸν πολιῆς ἔκτοσθε θαλάσσης
δικτύῳ ἐξέρυσαν πολυωπῷ· οἱ δέ τε πάντες
κύμαθ' ἁλὸς ποθέοντες ἐπὶ ψαμάθοισι κέχυνται·
τῶν μέν τ' Ἠέλιος φαέθων ἐξείλετο θυμόν·

(But he saw them, one and all in their numbers, lying fallen in their blood and in the dust, like fish whom the fishermen

have taken in their net with many holes, and dragged out
onto the hollow beach from the gray sea, and all of them
lie piled on the sand, needing the restless salt water;
but Helios, the shining Sun, bakes the life out of them.)

Nameless bodies unceremoniously cut down—we are invited
by this simile to look at them but not to sympathize with
them.

In general, the poet takes pains to recount the deaths of
those who have abused Odysseus or been disloyal. The three
suitors who struck or attempted to strike the old beggar, Antinoos, Eurymachos, and Ktesippos, are singled out. The first
two are killed by Odysseus himself to begin the slaughter.
The death of the third at Philoitios' hands ends the spear
fight proper. The disloyal serving women, twelve unnamed
women, are made to clean the hall (435–56) and are then
strung up by Telemachus (462–73). Instead of putting them
to the sword as instructed (443), he uses a ship's cable (465)
for the purpose. Throughout the poem ships have provided
for Odysseus a means of escape and victory over his enemies. The detail of the ship's cable here continues that motif.
Our last glimpse of these women is the pitiless line 473:

ἤσπαιρον δὲ πόδεσσι μίνυνθά περ, οὔ τι μάλα δήν.

(They struggled with their feet for a little, not very long.)

Melantho is certainly among them, though she is not named.
She perhaps did not have to be because the harshest punish-
ment is meted out last to Melanthios, her male counterpart.
Her punishment in some sense is subsumed in his (475–77):

τοῦ δ᾿ ἀπὸ μὲν ῥῖνάς τε καὶ οὔατα νηλέϊ χαλκῷ
τάμνον, μήδεά τ᾿ ἐξέρυσαν, κυσὶν ὠμὰ δάσασθαι,
χεῖράς τ᾿ ἠδὲ πόδας κόπτον κεκοτηότι θυμῷ.

(They cut off, with the pitiless bronze, his nose and his ears,
tore off his private parts and gave them to the dogs to feed on
raw, and lopped off his hands and feet, in fury of anger.)

This is extremely harsh, but then there is nothing more despicable than a disloyal servant. Odysseus takes no joy in the slaughter nor does he allow Eurykleia to cry out in triumph (407–18). Rather he views it and the punishment of the servants, his call for fire and brimstone suggests (493–94), as a necessary cleansing of the evil in his house.

Antinoos' death constitutes a particularly fine example of Homer's descriptive technique, in this case artfully recalling his earlier behavior in the poem. As the ringleader it is, of course, highly appropriate that Antinoos die first. We had last heard from him in the previous book (21.287–310) where, under the influence himself, he had accused the beggar of being drunk and ruining the feast, like the centaurs at the Lapith wedding. He is struck here then, most appropriately, in the throat as he is about to drink wine from a golden goblet (8–21). In addition, the general setting is one of eating and drinking, more specifically, a feast connected with the contest of the bow and the winning of Penelope's hand. Antinoos' last act, true to form, is a literal upsetting of the dinner table (19–21), a table that he had long abused by his flouting of Odysseus' house and the proper modes of eating and drinking.

Preparing his audience for what he plans to tell, the poet carefully inserts a strong reminder of Laertes into this book. Melanthios has found Laertes' old shield, which is suffering from dry rot but still serviceable, and is bringing it out when Eumaios and Philoitios waylay him (180–87). The shield well represents the old man's condition and reminds us of his absence from the palace and from the fray. This passage brilliantly prepares for the battle in book twenty-four, where not only is Laertes not absent, he takes the lead in the fight.

This book of harsh, swift retribution closes on a familiar domestic note. Summoned by Eurykleia, all the serving women crowd around Odysseus, kissing him and making much of him (495–501), much as they had greeted Telemachus on his return (17.33–35). These lines lead nicely into the twenty-third book, the focus of which is the recognition between Penelope and Odysseus.

BOOK TWENTY-THREE

Book twenty-three is Penelope's book. By its close we realize that she is the only woman for Odysseus, that she is his true counterpart. Homer has created a very memorable recognition;[8] he eschews the running embrace of filmdom to portray a more complex and believable encounter. Though Odysseus and Penelope know one another, they are, after twenty years apart, virtual strangers. Penelope, in particular, suddenly finds herself expected to welcome home her long-lost husband. It is a considerable adjustment, to say the least. Odysseus, by contrast, has the advantage, for he has been on Ithaca for several days and knows the situation from the inside.

The poet uses the opening scene with Eurykleia (1–84) to portray Penelope's nervous uncertainty and confusion.[9] Her immediate and natural reaction on being awakened from a happy sleep to the news that Odysseus is home and has killed the suitors is angry disbelief (11–24). When Eurykleia explains that he was the stranger, Penelope rejoices (31–33), but then asks pointedly how one man could have killed so many (35–38). To Eurykleia's description of the slaughter, she responds: "it must be the work of the gods; Odysseus is dead" (59–68). Eurykleia counters with the scar, which she recognized while washing his feet (73–75). With not a little touch of sarcasm, Penelope suggests that gods can manage scars too (81–82):

[8] On Penelope in this scene, see also Murnaghan, *Disguise and Recognition in the "Odyssey,"* 139–47.

[9] On Penelope's complex state of mind leading up to the recognition, see Whitman, *Homer and the Heroic Tradition,* 303–4.

μαῖα φίλη, χαλεπόν σε θεῶν αἰειγενετάων
δήνεα εἴρυσθαι, μάλα περ πολύϊδριν ἐοῦσαν·

(Nurse dear, it would be very hard for you to unravel the
   designs
of the gods everlasting, even though you are very clever.)

(My trans.)

As Penelope descends to see the one who has killed the suitors, she has all her guards up. She still needs time to adjust.

The recognition scene (85–240) concentrates on Penelope.
She is expected to react; Odysseus uncharacteristically says
nothing, but sits waiting (89–92). The focus is on Penelope's
agonized silence. Telemachus breaks the silence that neither
of his parents can by rebuking his mother. At this point one
would expect his father out of gallantry, if nothing else, to
intercede and point out that they have signs just between the
two of them. It is, most strikingly, Penelope who says this
(105ff.), and in so doing she suggests that some things are
better done without children present. Odysseus takes the
hint, and there follows a short scene (113–52) in which he
proposes a stratagem to buy some time to deal with the relatives of the suitors. His plan cleverly gives Telemachus and
the others something to do, namely simulate a noisy wedding feast, and gets them out of the way so that he and Penelope can be reunited. Here the wedding motif reaches its
conclusion. Odysseus has completed the contest for the hand
of the queen and, as a wedding feast goes on in the background, he and Penelope will, after twenty years, again be
together as husband and wife.

The focus is now momentarily on Odysseus. Eurynome
bathes him (153–55) and Athena transforms him (156ff.), just
as she had in his first meeting with Nausicaa in the sixth
book. Lines 157–61 are, in fact, identical to lines 230–34 of
book six. There the effect on Nausicaa was immediate and
Odysseus clearly expects the same from Penelope here. But
Penelope is no young and inexperienced Nausicaa. Though

Homer does not describe it, she clearly makes no reaction to this marvelous transformation. This explains Odysseus' impatient scolding of Penelope at 166 and following. He ends with a peremptory invitation to bed if she is of a mind (171–72).

She now tests him by ordering Eurykleia to make up out in the hall the very bed that he had built. The language of this short speech (174–80) deserves careful appreciation. "Strange man" (δαιμόνι᾽), her first word in line 174, throws back his first word of rebuke to her at line 166 and here suggests her independence. The spondaic fifth foot cadence in two successive lines (176–77) conveys her deliberate calculation as she baits her trap.[10] The emphasis in three successive lines on "solid," "well-built" (πυκινόν, 177; ἐϋσταθέος, 178; πυκινόν, 179) completes the trap by teasing Odysseus with that quality which most marks the bed that he built for their marriage chamber so many years ago. Odysseus falls for it and describes their bed, the sure sign that Penelope exacts to accept him. She alone in the poem tricks him into giving ironclad proof of his identity. She is truly his wife.

What better token of recognition between husband and wife than the bed that they shared. This particular bed all but completes the tree imagery within the poem and symbolizes, by being rooted in the center of the house, the solidity of the marriage and the house. Trees, particularly the olive tree, have been symbols of life throughout the poem. Odysseus preserves himself at the end of book five by burying himself in the leaves under an olive. He uses an olive stake to put out the eye of Polyphemos. He grabs on for dear life at the end of the twelfth book to a fig tree to escape Charybdis. At the opening of book thirteen, an olive is prominent at the

---

[10] The normal practice at the end of the hexameter line is for the fifth foot to be a dactyl followed by a spondee in the sixth foot, i.e., long short short, long long. To end a line with two successive spondees (long long, long long), that is, four long syllables in a row, is unusual; it perceptibly slows down the line and is sometimes used, as here, for special effect.

head of the bay as he arrives in Ithaca. The olive is a particularly long-lived tree and a valuable commodity in the Mediterranean world. It is common to measure the value of a
property by the number of olive trees on it. The olive is a
natural symbol, therefore, for life and the continuance of
property from one generation to the next. Finally, Homer
will use trees in just this way in the last book, where the trees
of the estate become the token of recognition between Odysseus and his father. The rooted olive, then, is most appropriate for Odysseus' and Penelope's bed.

Certain critics, ancient and modern, have wished to end
the poem at line 296—and so to bed. But to do this is to lose
sight of the fact that the poem is not primarily about the reunion of a husband and his wife; rather, it tells of the return
of a king and his recovery of his house in the widest sense of
that word. Furthermore, the reunion is far more than simply
sexual; Odysseus and Penelope have a lot of catching up to
do. Before making love they embrace for a long time (240–
41), and Odysseus shares with Penelope the one thing she
really must in fairness know at once, namely that he must
leave again soon (248–87). After making love, they tell each
other of their experiences (301–9). In sharing they become
kindred spirits.[11]

The transition from the recognition and reunion with Penelope is made swiftly at lines 344ff. It is prepared for by
Odysseus' discussion with Telemachus about the relatives of
the suitors (117ff.) and by his disclosure to Penelope that he
must soon leave (247ff.). The ruse of the wedding party (131–
51, 297–99) and Penelope's account of the suitors (302–5) de-
signedly keep before us the doings outside the palace and aid

_____

[11] Lines 310–43 appear to me a certain interpolation. Lines 301–9 have
made the point and in keeping with the emphasis of this book have stressed
the actions and reactions of Penelope. She speaks first (302–5) and then lis-
tens to Odysseus with delight before sleeping (308–9). Lines 310–43 place an
undue emphasis on Odysseus. But the strongest reason for regarding these
lines as an interpolation is a stylistic one. They are cast insistently into indirect discourse; the manner is foreign to Homer.

the transition. Athena, after giving Penelope and Odysseus one long night to enjoy (241–46), a night that belongs, like the book itself, primarily to Penelope, brings the dawn (347–48) and with it the time for Odysseus to act and for Penelope to withdraw into her upper chamber, the passive woman once more (364–65). Athena's particular action in the last two lines of the book "shrouding in night" (νυκτὶ κατακρύψασα, 372, a unique phrase) Odysseus and his band artfully leads into the twenty-fourth book, which begins with a scene in the underworld.

Book twenty-three brings to completion the motif of the contest for the hand of the princess first introduced with the Phaeacians in books five to eight. The entire sequence begins in book five (388ff.) with a simile comparing the shipwrecked Odysseus' joy at catching sight of land to children's joy at seeing their father recover from a deathlike illness, and ends in book twenty-three (232ff.) with a simile comparing Penelope's joy at recovering Odysseus to the joy of shipwrecked sailors at seeing land. There can be no doubt that the second simile deliberately recalls and balances the first.[12] Moreover, the major events in these respective "contests" form a ring composition. In Phaeacia the order is: (1) shipwreck and simile; (2) bath and rejuvenation by Athena; (3) Odysseus bests the young men; (4) he identifies himself to the Phaeacians. The order is reversed in books twenty-one to twenty-three: (4) Odysseus identifies himself to the suitors; (3) he kills the suitors; (2) bath and rejuvenation by Athena; (1) simile of shipwrecked sailors. Odysseus' story begins with his winning the hand of a princess whom he cannot have and ends with his winning the hand of his rightful queen. His son precedes and his father follows; this arrangement clearly binds the poem together and affirms the central importance of the house as defined by the continuance of the male line.

[12] Austin, *Archery at the Dark of the Moon*, 141.

B O O K   T W E N T Y - F O U R

Book twenty-four provides a fitting *and necessary* close to the story.[13] The hero has returned home, successfully taken his revenge upon the suitors, and been reunited with his wife. There remains only one member of his family with whom he has not been reunited, his father, Laertes. Not surprisingly then, the final book brings Odysseus and his father back together. This poem of self-discovery begins then with Odysseus' son and ends with his father, the two parameters, so to speak, of his existence. Moreover, since a controlling motif of the story has been the journey in search of identity, Odysseus can scarcely be completely himself until he identifies himself to his father and resumes the roles of son and heir.

The families of the suitors must also be reckoned with. They cannot simply ignore the murder of their sons; ancient custom required that they retaliate or at least seek recompense. Vengeance for relatives harmed or slain has been an important motif of the poem beginning with Poseidon's anger at Odysseus for the blinding of Polyphemos (1.68–75) and encompassing, of course, Odysseus' killing of the suitors, not least in revenge for their attempt to murder his only son, Telemachus. Theoklymenos fled from Argos to avoid being slain by the relatives of a man he had killed (15.272–76).

οὕτω τοι καὶ ἐγὼν ἐκ πατρίδος, ἄνδρα κατακτὰς
ἔμφυλον· πολλοὶ δὲ κασίγνητοί τε ἔται τε
Ἄργος ἀν᾽ ἱππόβοτον, μέγα δὲ κρατέουσιν Ἀχαιῶν.
τῶν ὑπαλευάμενος θάνατον καὶ κῆρα μέλαιναν
φεύγω

(So I too am out of my country, because I have killed
a man of my tribe, but he had many brothers and relatives

---

[13] On the ending in general, see Moulton, "The End of the *Odyssey*," and Wender, *The Last Scenes of the "Odyssey."* Many have found the ending of the poem "un-Homeric" and/or inept; Page, *The Homeric "Odyssey*," 101–36, and Kirk, *The Songs of Homer*, 244–51 are eloquent representatives of this position.

in horse-pasturing Argos, with great power among the
Achaians.
Avoiding death at the hands of these men and black doom, I am
a fugitive. . . .)

How much more has Odysseus to fear since he has killed the best young men, not only of Ithaca, but of the surrounding islands and nearby mainland? He perceives the problem and worries about it even before killing the suitors, for he taxes Athena with it at lines 41–43 of book twenty:

πρὸς δ᾽ ἔτι καὶ τόδε μεῖζον ἐνὶ φρεσὶ μερμηρίζω·
εἴ περ γὰρ κτείναιμι Διός τε σέθεν τε ἕκητι,
πῇ κεν ὑπεκπροφύγοιμι;

(And here is a still bigger problem that my heart is pondering.
Even if, by grace of Zeus and yourself, I kill them,
how shall I make my escape?)

And, almost immediately after killing the suitors, he expresses his concern to Telemachus (23.118–22):

καὶ γὰρ τίς θ᾽ ἕνα φῶτα κατακτείνας ἐνὶ δήμῳ,
ᾧ μὴ πολλοὶ ἔωσιν ἀοσσητῆρες ὀπίσσω,
φεύγει πηούς τε προλιπὼν καὶ πατρίδα γαῖαν·
ἡμεῖς δ᾽ ἕρμα πόληος ἀπέκταμεν, οἳ μέγ᾽ ἄριστοι
κούρων εἰν Ἰθάκῃ· τὰ δέ σε φράζεσθαι ἄνωγα.

(For when one has killed only one man in a community,
and then there are not many avengers to follow, even
so, he flees into exile, leaving kinsmen and country.
But we have killed what held the city together, the finest
young men in Ithaca. It is what I would have you consider.)

The problem is a real one and must be resolved, else the storyline will be left dangling and intolerably so. Homer realized this (though many of his critics have not)[14] and devoted

---

[14] Page in his attack on the end of the *Odyssey* as an appended continuation (*The Homeric "Odyssey,"* 101–36) fails to consider this point.

much of the final book to smoothing over the situation in Ithaca.

Book twenty-four begins, as the poem as a whole had, with an apparent digression. Instead of taking us to the farm of Laertes, as the end of book twenty-three had naturally led us to expect, Homer depicts Hermes leading the ghosts of the suitors to the underworld. There they find the spirits of Achilles and Agamemnon in conversation. Gathered around Agamemnon are the souls of his followers who were foully murdered with him in the house of Aigisthos (21–22). The inclusion of these innocent victims here places the suitors, by the contrast, in an unfavorable light. The friendly conversation of the two spirits concerns death with honor. In fact, Agamemnon's account of the death and burial of Achilles with the highest honors (35–97) immediately precedes and comments on Amphimedon's account of the death of the suitors (121–90). Amphimedon in vain tries to elicit sympathy from Agamemnon (186–90).

> ὣς ἡμεῖς, Ἀγάμεμνον, ἀπωλόμεθ᾽, ὧν ἔτι καὶ νῦν
> σώματ᾽ ἀκηδέα κεῖται ἐνὶ μεγάροις Ὀδυσῆος·
> οὐ γάρ πω ἴσασι φίλοι κατὰ δώμαθ᾽ ἑκάστου,
> οἵ κ᾽ ἀπονίψαντες μέλανα βρότον ἐξ ὠτειλέων
> κατθέμενοι γοάοιεν· ὃ γὰρ γέρας ἐστὶ θανόντων.

(So, Agamemnon, we were destroyed, and still at this moment
our bodies are lying uncared-for in the halls of Odysseus;
for our people in the house of each man know nothing of this,
they who would have washed away from our wounds the black
  blood,
and laid us out and mourned us; for this is the right of the
  perished.)

Agamemnon can of course have no sympathy, and his reaction shows it—he utters not one word of solace to Amphimedon (in fact, he says nothing to him), but simply exclaims on the good fortune of Odysseus in having Penelope as his wife. This tribute to Penelope fittingly accords her a last moment of emphasis in this final book. At the same time, the dismissal of the suitors' fate by implication as justly deserved colors importantly the hearer's response to the end of the poem. We are being prepared to accept as reasonable that the suitors' families (with, to be sure, the aid of Zeus) should forgive and forget. This opening scene in the underworld also, by shifting abruptly away from the human level of action, prepares the way for the intervention of Zeus and Athena, which closes this book and the epic.

These first 204 lines in at least one other way promote a mood of reconciliation. The very friendly conversation between Agamemnon and Achilles comes as a considerable surprise, or should, to anyone who knows the *Iliad*. In that poem Achilles and Agamemnon can scarcely tolerate one another, exchange some extremely bitter insults, and are never reconciled. The present scene shows that even the bitterest enemies can make it up and foreshadows the rapprochement between Odysseus and the families of the suitors. Thus, this scene, while it seems to digress, forwards in a significant way one of the primary subjects of this book.

The first scene also concludes several important elements of the poem. It ends the story of Agamemnon, a story that has been constantly present to Odysseus and Telemachus, as a warning to the one not to trust women and as an example to the other of how the son of a hero ought to behave. It also completes the eleventh book, the memorable visit to the underworld, by portraying the ghosts of that book as learning of Odysseus' successful homecoming and rejoicing in it. They know the end of the expedition in which they participated while they were alive. This is an important element contributing to the sense of closure that this book achieves. In fact, the poet intentionally seems to bring to a close both the *Iliad* and the *Odyssey* in this book—the *Iliad*, by the account of Achilles' funeral; the *Odyssey*, by restoring Odysseus to his rightful place in Ithaca.

Agamemnon's praise of Penelope (192–202) also provides a disarmingly natural transition back to human affairs and to the events on Ithaca (205). Odysseus and his companions arrive at the steading of Laertes, and Odysseus goes out alone into the orchard in search of his father. He finds the old man working amidst the trees dressed in a sorry fashion. Notice, however, that even in his squalor Laertes' dress suggests his former heroic valor, for the articles of clothing that he wears, particularly the patched "leggings" (κνημῖδας, 229: everywhere else in Homer the word signifies greaves) and the goatskin "head gear" (κυνέην, 231: elsewhere used to refer to helmets) recall specifically pieces of armor. Note too that the setting in the orchard brings together and naturally completes the tree imagery in the poem.

Many have criticized this initial meeting between Odysseus and Laertes as heartless;[15] they argue that, instead of deceiving his father, it would have been better for Odysseus to have revealed himself in a straightforward manner. To have made him do this would have been in fact to make him behave in an un-Odysseus-like manner. Caution and dissimulation are part and parcel of his character. Lacking them, Odysseus is not Odysseus, and he would have been unrecognizable to his father. Homer is not without feeling. The entire deception is brief, about 80 lines (240–320), Odysseus himself is deeply pained by it (318–19), and immediately says that it is he, home at last, in the twentieth year (321–22). Laertes' caution equals that of his son; instead of rejoicing, he asks for proof: "Tell me at once a sure sign" (329). Odysseus shows him the scar of his boyhood and then, as the sign special to his father, recalls an experience that they alone had shared and that epitomizes their relationship (336–42):

εἰ δ᾽ ἄγε τοι καὶ δένδρε᾽ ἐϋκτιμένην κατ᾽ ἀλωὴν
εἴπω, ἅ μοί ποτ᾽ ἔδωκας, ἐγὼ δ᾽ ᾔτεόν σε ἕκαστα

---

[15] Page, The Homeric "Odyssey," 111–12, first and foremost. For a recent refutation of Page's views, see J. H. Finley, Homer's "Odyssey," 224–33.

παιδνὸς ἐών, κατὰ κῆπον ἐπισπόμενος· διὰ δ᾽αὐτῶν
ἱκνεύμεσθα, σὺ δ᾽ ὠνόμασας καὶ ἔειπες ἕκαστα.
ὄγχνας μοι δῶκας τρισκαίδεκα καὶ δέκα μηλέας,
συκέας τεσσαράκοντ᾽· ὄρχους δέ μοι ὧδ᾽ ὀνόμηνας
δώσειν πεντήκοντα

(Or come then, let me tell you of the trees in the well-worked
orchard, which you gave me once. I asked you of each one,
when I was a child, following you through the garden. We went
among the trees, and you named them all and told me what
    each one
was, and you gave me thirteen pear trees, and ten apple trees,
and forty fig trees; and so also you named the fifty
vines you would give. . . .)

Laertes faints at the realization that his son and heir has at
last come home. When he revives after a moment, he has
completely changed. No longer is he so overwhelmed by
troubles that he has given up any desire to live. Now once
again he is actively concerned with living and acutely realizes
the central problem that faces them (353–54):

νῦν δ᾽ αἰνῶς δείδοικα κατὰ φρένα μὴ τάχα πάντες
ἐνθάδ᾽ ἐπέλθωσιν Ἰθακήσιοι.

(But now I am terribly afraid in my heart that speedily
the men of Ithaca [the suitors' relatives] may come against
    us. . . .)

The momentary faint and recovery is a death and rebirth
in miniature. In keeping with this, Laertes now has several
experiences that replicate those of this son. Most notably, he
is bathed and then Athena rejuvenates him by making him
"taller than before and thicker in appearance" (369). This
idea, though not precisely these words, has occurred four
times before in the poem, thrice of Odysseus (6.230, 8.20,
23.157) and once of Penelope (18.195). This action of Athena
helps to equate father and son. Laertes too now has his loyal
servants—Dolios and his sons, who come to swear their loy-

alty (387–405)—as Odysseus had had Eumaios and Philoitios. Finally, in the battle that ensues, Laertes throws the first spear, killing Eupeithes, the father of Antinoos and the ring-leader of the suitors' relatives (521–25); this act directly par-allels Odysseus' killing of Antinoos first at the beginning of the slaughter of the suitors. At this point Laertes has momen-tarily taken the lead, that is to say he has assumed Odysseus' role—father and son have become all but one.

The final scenes of the poem bring the denouement swiftly. Here, in ending, the poet deliberately recalls scenes from the opening books of the epic. They remind us of what the situation was and emphasize how much it has changed. In books one and two Athena's intervention with Zeus on behalf of Odysseus led to an assembly in which the suitors were asked in vain to give up their insolent behavior in the halls of Odysseus. Here in the twenty-fourth book an assem-bly in which the relatives of the suitors are asked in vain to give up their desire for revenge (421–71) motivates Athena to intercede with Zeus, this time, strikingly, on behalf of both parties (473–76). And when Athena intervenes in the action after Laertes has killed Eupeithes, her words are addressed to both sides, but more, the turn of phrase "men of Ithaca" (Ἰθακήσιοι, 531) suggests, to the attackers. Her purpose, for the first time in the entire poem, is to aid someone other than Odysseus or a member of his family. Not fully under-standing the change, Odysseus, now wholly the king in his own domain, swoops to attack like an eagle (538), the bird of kings and the particular bird of Zeus, and Zeus himself must restrain him with his thunderbolt (539), so great has he be-come. Athena then speaks to him for the last time and tells him to stop. Our last picture is of Athena in the guise of Men-tor settling the truce; this too brings us full circle by remind-ing us of how the poem began, i.e., with Athena disguised as Mentes coming to the palace to visit Telemachus.

This book shows us the rejuvenation and reinvolvement of Laertes as the first four had depicted Telemachus' coming of age. Each undergoes a transformation: the one a death and rebirth symbolized by his momentary fainting spell, the other a growth to manhood on his journey. Athena aids materially in the change in each case. These transformations match, but in briefer, less extreme form, experiences of Odysseus that form the central part of the poem. He, after all, has performed the greatest exploits of which a hero is capable, not least of which is to conquer death in the only ways a mortal can, by accepting it for what it is and by achieving undying fame in song. Each becomes the sort of man who can truly be the son or the father of a great hero such as Odysseus is, namely a hero himself. One of the major unifying aspects of the poem has been the similar experiences that these three men have had. Each has made a journey, the goal of which was the palace of Odysseus and the reuniting of the royal family. Homer thus brings all three together at the close: this is the true goal, *telos*, of the poem—the three united, armed, and prepared to do battle. Laertes rejoices (514–15):

τίς νύ μοι ἡμέρη ἥδε, θεοὶ φίλοι; ἦ μάλα χαίρω·
υἱός θ' υἱωνός τ' ἀρετῆς πέρι δῆριν ἔχουσι.

(What a day this is for me, dear gods! Truly I rejoice.
My son and my son's son are competing in valor.) (My trans.)

The *Odyssey* as the Conclusion to the Story of the Heroes at Troy

HOMER DESIGNED the *Odyssey* as the conclusion to the story of the heroes at Troy. Whether or not this is the same Homer as the one who composed the *Iliad*, and I for one think he is, hardly matters; the intent of this artist is clearly to bring both poems to a close.[1] This poem sees Odysseus, the last of the heroes from Troy, safely home. It also includes for good measure an account of the return of Menelaos, the next to the last of the returnees. "All the others, as many as escaped death, were at home" (1.11–12). The voyage of Odysseus advertises itself in the opening verses as the return of all returns, and during it the hero makes the ultimate journey, to the underworld. There can logically never be another return equal to this, and Homer uses the Phaeacians to underline this point. With the transformation of their ship to stone in book thirteen, an era has past. Troy is past and heroes won't make returns of this kind ever again.

As a way of rounding out the *Iliad*, the poet carefully presents us in the *Odyssey* with the major heroes of that poem.[2] In company with Telemachus, we encounter first Nestor at

---

[1] Schein, *The Mortal Hero*, 37–38.

[2] It has often been noted too that the poet of the *Odyssey* carefully avoids stories already told in the *Iliad*; rather he recounts complementary episodes. For a clear account of this, see Lattimore, *The "Odyssey" of Homer*, 18–20. I am of the opinion that this is a deliberate device on the part of the poet in order to keep both tales before us, while avoiding the mere repetition of episodes already told in the first poem. I have, the reader will gather, no doubt of the *Iliad*'s priority. Janko's recent study, *Homer, Hesiod and the Hymns*, provides support for this belief.

Pylos (book 3), and then Menelaos and Helen at Sparta (book 4). Moreover, the poet brings to conclusion in book eleven the stories of the three greatest heroes, Agamemnon, Achilles, and Ajax. We also receive an elaborate account of Achilles' funeral (24.36–94) and, most significantly for our sense of the story of Troy coming to a close, twice hear about the wooden horse and the fall of Troy (4.271–89; 8.499–520). Finally, as he ends the *Odyssey*, Homer gives us in the twenty-fourth book a most amicable exchange between the two archrivals of the *Iliad*, who are never truly reconciled in that poem, Agamemnon and Achilles. In book twenty-four of the *Odyssey*, the story of the wrath and the story of the return reach their ends.[3]

[3] On the *Odyssey* as making a claim to surpass the *Iliad*, i.e., as in competition with it, see A. T. Edwards, *Achilles in the "Odyssey,"* 89–93; cf. also Nagy, *The Best of the Achaeans*, 35–40.

SUGGESTIONS FOR FURTHER READING

THESE SUGGESTIONS are divided into two parts, the first intended for Greekless readers, the second for students reading the poem in Greek. Obviously the books in the first part will be useful to all readers. The following books constitute of necessity a highly selective list; there are many other worthwhile books on Homer and the *Odyssey*. I have chosen these few on the grounds that they seem to me especially useful for beginning students or those near the beginning. Publication information can be found in the list of Articles and Books Cited.

I

Clarke, Howard W., *The Art of the "Odyssey"*—a sensitive introduction to the poem.

Finley, Moses I., *The World of Odysseus*—a helpful account of Homeric society.

Lord, Albert B., *The Singer of Tales*—the fullest statement of what an oral singer is.

Page, Denys, *Folktales in Homer's "Odyssey"*—a useful introduction to the folktale elements in the poem.

Stanford, W. B., *The Ulysses Theme: The Adaptability of a Traditional Hero*—traces the figure of Odysseus through Western literature.

II

Austin, Norman, *Archery at the Dark of the Moon: Poetic Problems in Homer's "Odyssey"*—argues sensibly for Homer's complexity of thought and feeling.

Fenik, Bernard, *Studies in the "Odyssey"*—an important examination of the poet's predilection for certain types of scenes, combining the methods of oral poetry studies with a keen awareness of continental, especially German, scholarship.

Murnaghan, Sheila, *Disguise and Recognition in the "Odyssey"*—a good recent treatment of this important theme.

Page, Denys, *The Homeric "Odyssey"*—a most important study representing an old-fashioned but still influential "analytic" approach to the poem.

Parry, Adam, Introduction to Milman Parry's *The Making of Homeric Verse*—the best short summary in English of the Homeric question, oral theory, and related issues.

Parry, Milman, *The Making of Homeric Verse*—the collected works of the scholar who first made the scholarly world come to grips with the orality of Homer's poetry.

Stanford, W. B., *The "Odyssey" of Homer*, 2nd. ed.—this is the standard commentary in English; but see now *A Commentary on Homer's "Odyssey"* (in progress) by Alfred Heubeck et al.

Whitman, Cedric H., *Homer and the Heroic Tradition*—still one of the best general books on Homer; it emphasizes the *Iliad*, but has a good chapter on the *Odyssey*.

For further bibliography, see the surveys by James P. Holoka in *Classical World* 73 (1979): 69–150, and by Mark W. Edwards in *Oral Tradition* 1 (1986): 171–229, 3 (1988): 11–60. Howard Clarke, *Homer's Readers*, provides a good history of the ways Homer has been read.

ARTICLES AND BOOKS CITED

Amory, Anne. "The Gates of Horn and Ivory." *Yale Classical Studies* 20 (1966): 3–57.

———. "The Reunion of Odysseus and Penelope." In *Essays on the "Odyssey,"* edited by Charles H. Taylor, Jr., 100–121. Bloomington: Indiana University Press, 1963.

Anderson, William S. "Calypso and Elysium." In *Essays on the "Odyssey,"* edited by Charles H. Taylor, Jr., 83–86. Bloomington: Indiana University Press, 1963.

Austin, Norman. *Archery at the Dark of the Moon: Poetic Problems in Homer's "Odyssey."* Berkeley: University of California Press, 1975.

Beye, Charles R. *The "Iliad," the "Odyssey," and the Epic Tradition.* New York: Doubleday, 1966.

Byre, Calvin S. "Penelope and the Suitors before Odysseus: *Odyssey* 18.158–303." *American Journal of Philology* 109 (1988): 159–73.

Clarke, Howard W. *The Art of the "Odyssey."* Englewood Cliffs, N.J.: Prentice-Hall, 1967.

———. *Homer's Readers.* Newark: University of Delaware Press, 1980.

———. "Telemachus and the *Telemacheia.*" *American Journal of Philology* 84 (1963): 129–45.

Clay, Jenny Strauss. *The Wrath of Athena.* Princeton: Princeton University Press, 1984.

Detienne, Marcel, and Jean-Pierre Vernant. *Cunning Intelligence in Greek Society.* Translated by Janet Lloyd. Atlantic Highlands, N.J.: Humanities Press, 1978.

Dimock, George E., Jr. "The Name of Odysseus." In *Essays on the "Odyssey,"* edited by Charles H. Taylor, Jr., 54–72. Bloomington: Indiana University Press, 1963.

Edwards, Anthony T. *Achilles in the "Odyssey."* Meisenheim am Glan: Hain, 1985.

Edwards, Mark W. *Homer, Poet of the "Iliad."* Baltimore: The Johns Hopkins University Press, 1987.

———. "Homer and Oral Tradition: The Formula, Parts I, II." *Oral Tradition* 1 (1986): 171–229, 3 (1988): 11–60.

154   ARTICLES AND BOOKS CITED

Fenik, Bernard. *Studies in the "Odyssey."* Hermes Einzelschriften 30. Wiesbaden: F. Steiner, 1974.

Finnegan, Ruth. *Oral Poetry: Its Nature, Significance and Social Context.* Cambridge: Cambridge University Press, 1977.

Finley, John H., Jr. *Homer's "Odyssey."* Cambridge, Mass.: Harvard University Press, 1978.

Finley, Moses I. *The World of Odysseus.* 2nd ed., rev. New York: Viking Press, 1978.

Frame, Douglas. *The Myth of Return in Early Greek Epic.* New Haven: Yale University Press, 1978.

Goold, G. P. "The Nature of Homeric Composition." *Illinois Classical Studies* 2 (1977): 1–34.

———. "The Removal of the Arms in the *Odyssey.*" In *Studies in Honour of T. B. L. Webster*, 122–29. Bristol: Bristol University Press, 1986.

Griffin, Jasper. *Homer on Life and Death.* Oxford: Clarendon Press, 1980.

———. *Homer, The "Odyssey."* Cambridge: Cambridge University Press, 1987.

Hainsworth, J. B. "The Criticism of an Oral Homer." *Journal of Hellenic Studies* 90 (1970): 90–97.

Heubeck, Alfred, Stephanie West, and J. B. Hainsworth. *A Commentary on Homer's "Odyssey."* Vol. 1. Oxford: Clarendon Press, 1988.

Heubeck, Alfred and Arie Hoekstra. *A Commentary on Homer's "Odyssey."* Vol. 2. Oxford: Clarendon Press, 1989.

Heubeck, Alfred, J. Russo, and M. Fernandez-Galiano. *A Commentary on Homer's "Odyssey."* Vol. 3. Oxford: Clarendon Press (forthcoming).

Holoka, James P. "Homeric Studies 1971–1977." *Classical World* 73 (1979): 69–150.

Janko, Richard. *Homer, Hesiod and the Hymns: Diachronic Development in Epic Diction.* Cambridge: Cambridge University Press, 1982.

Kearns, Emily. "The Return of Odysseus: A Homeric Theoxeny." *Classical Quarterly* 32 (1982): 2–8.

Kirk, G. S. *Homer and the Oral Tradition.* Cambridge: Cambridge University Press, 1976.

———. *The Songs of Homer.* Cambridge: Cambridge University Press, 1962.

Kitto, H.D.F. *Poiesis: Structure and Thought*. Berkeley: University of California Press, 1966.

Lattimore, Richmond, "Nausikaa's Suitors." In *Studies Presented to Ben Edwin Perry*, 88–102. Urbana: University of Illinois Press, 1969.

———. trans. *The "Odyssey" of Homer*. New York: Harper and Row, 1965.

Levine, Daniel B. "*Odyssey* 18: Iros as Paradigm for the Suitors." *Classical Journal* 77 (1982): 200–204.

Lord, Albert B. *The Singer of Tales*. Cambridge, Mass.: Harvard University Press, 1960.

McLeod, Wallace. "The Bow and the Axes." In *Studies Presented to Sterling Dow on His Eightieth Birthday*, 203–10. Greek, Roman, and Byzantine Monograph 10. Durham, N.C.: 1984.

Moulton, Carroll. "The End of the *Odyssey*." *Greek, Roman and Byzantine Studies* 15 (1974): 153–69.

Murnaghan, Sheila M. *Disguise and Recognition in the "Odyssey."* Princeton: Princeton University Press, 1987.

Nagy, Gregory. *The Best of the Achaeans*. Baltimore: The Johns Hopkins University Press, 1977.

Owen, E. T. *The Story of the "Iliad."* Toronto: Clarke, Irwin and Company Limited, 1946.

Page, Denys. *Folktales in Homer's "Odyssey."* Cambridge, Mass.: Harvard University Press, 1973.

———. *The Homeric "Odyssey."* Oxford: Clarendon Press, 1955.

Parry, Adam. "Have We Homer's *Iliad*?" *Yale Classical Studies* 20 (1966): 177–216.

Parry, Milman. *The Making of Homeric Verse*. Edited by Adam Parry. Oxford: Clarendon Press, 1971.

Podlecki, A. J. "Omens in the *Odyssey*." *Greece & Rome* 14 (1967): 12–23.

Pucci, Pietro. *Odysseus Polutropos: Intertextual Readings in the "Odyssey" and the "Iliad."* Ithaca: Cornell University Press, 1987.

Redfield, James. *Nature and Culture in the "Iliad."* Chicago: The University of Chicago Press, 1975.

Rose, Gilbert P. "The Unfriendly Phaeacians." *Transactions of the American Philological Association* 100 (1969): 387–406.

Russo, Joseph. "Interview and Aftermath: Dream, Fantasy, and Intuition in *Odyssey* 19 and 20." *American Journal of Philology* 103 (1982): 4–18.

Schein, Seth L. *The Mortal Hero*. Berkeley: University of California Press, 1984.

Segal, Charles P. "*Kleos* and Its Ironies in the *Odyssey*." *L'Antiquité Classique* 52 (1983): 22–47.

Stanford, W. B. *The "Odyssey" of Homer*. 2nd ed. 2 vols. London: Macmillan, 1958.

———. *The Ulysses Theme: A Study in the Adaptability of a Traditional Hero*. 2nd. ed. Oxford: Basil Blackwell & Mott, 1983.

Van Nortwick, Thomas. "Penelope and Nausicaa." *Transactions of the American Philological Association* 109 (1979): 269–76.

Wender, Dorothea. *The Last Scenes of the "Odyssey."* Mnemosyne Supplement 52. Leiden: Brill, 1978.

West, M. L. *Fragmenta Hesiodea*. Oxford: Clarendon Press, 1967.

Whitman, Cedric H. *Homer and the Heroic Tradition*. Cambridge, Mass.: Harvard University Press, 1958.

Woodhouse, W. J. *The Composition of Homer's "Odyssey."* Oxford: Clarendon Press, 1930.

INDEX OF NAMES AND PLACES

Eumaios, 78, 80, 84, 85–88, 90–92,
95, 97, 101, 102, 103, 113, 114,
120, 123, 128–29, 131, 134, 145
Eupeithes, 145, 146
Euryalos, 52
Eurykleia, 11, 15, 22, 110–11, 115–
17, 123, 134, 135–36, 137
Eurymachos, 10, 11, 13–14, 92, 97,
101, 105, 109, 123, 128, 133
Eurynome, 136
Eurytos, 125

family, 4, 22, 33, 36, 45, 53–54, 79,
80, 89, 95
fathers and sons, 3–4, 10, 11, 16–17,
23, 46, 78–79, 81n, 89, 91, 94, 97,
126, 138, 139–40, 144–45, 147
females, 47, 56, 64, 66
fire, symbolic of victory, 109–10,
113, 121

gods, 4–5, 29, 41, 49, 75, 76, 82, 94,
99, 102; council of, 29–30; trivial-
ity of their existence, 32
guest/host relationship, 3, 8, 11, 18,
22, 24, 27, 30, 48, 53, 62, 86, 88,
89, 93, 98, 102, 125, 132, 134

Halitherses, 12–14
Hector, 112–13
Helen, 22, 23, 24–25, 46, 89, 150
Helios, 56
Hephaistos, 52
Herakles, 73, 125
Hermes, 6, 11, 27, 29, 30, 31, 32, 34,
65, 66, 73, 142
Hesiod, 73
Homeric question, xiii

Idomeneus, 113
Iliad, 3, 7n, 15, 51, 54n, 71, 110,
112–13, 120, 124n, 143, 149–50
Ino, 32–33
Iphitos, 125
Iros, 98, 105–6, 109, 127

journey(s), xi, 3–4, 11, 46, 57, 78,

140, 146–47; of Odysseus, 27, 32,
47, 55, 66, 68, 70n, 75, 79–81, 101,
149; of Telemachus, 13, 16, 21, 84,
101

Kikones, 55, 58, 59, 63
Kimmerians, 67
Kleos, 9, 31–32, 50, 58, 59, 84
Ktesippos, 132, 133
Kythera, 60

Lapiths, 127, 134
Laertes, 3, 8, 11, 57, 87, 107, 122,
134, 138, 140, 141, 143–47
Laestrygonians, 56, 64, 65, 67
Leodes, 123, 132
Leokritos, 12–14, 132
Leukothea, 27, 32–33
Lotos Eaters, 55, 58, 60

marriage, 28, 36–37, 38, 41, 42–43,
52, 89, 108, 119, 128, 137. *See also*
wedding; wooing
Medon, 132
Melanthios, 98, 101, 102, 119, 121,
131, 133–34
Melantho, 98, 101n, 105, 109, 111,
133
Menelaos, 4, 18–19, 21, 22–26, 46,
86, 88, 89, 100, 149–50
Mentes, 4, 7, 8, 10, 146
Mentor, 4, 12–14, 17, 20, 21, 79,
131, 132, 146
Meriones, 51n
me tis, 61
metis, 61
Minos, 73
moly, 66, 67
mortality/immortality, xi–xii, 4, 27,
31–32, 50, 74
murderers, pollution of, 82, 90

Nausicaa, 28, 36–46, 47, 49, 52, 86n,
89, 108n, 136
Nestor, 4, 16–21, 24, 41, 46, 62, 89,
90, 149
nostos, 5, 6, 43, 59n, 89. *See also* return home